Collected Poems 1969–1982

COLLECTED POEMS
1969-1982

Constance Hunting

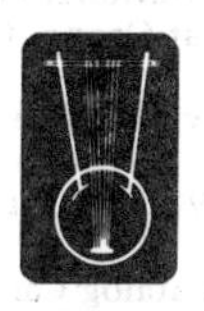

THE NATIONAL POETRY FOUNDATION
University of Maine at Orono 1983

"To a Patron" is taken from the *Letters* of Aubrey Beardsley; "Emergent Occasions" is taken from the *Journals* of Mary Shelley; "Ornithological" is taken from the *Observer's Book of Cornish Birds*; "American Notes" is taken for the most part from *The Illustrated London News*, April 28, 1894.

Published by The National Poetry Foundation
University of Maine at Orono, Orono, Maine 04469

Printed by The University of Maine at Orono Printing Office

Library of Congress Catalog Card Number: 83-62145
ISBN: 0-915032-19-8 paper

CONTENTS

CITY PARK: SPRING

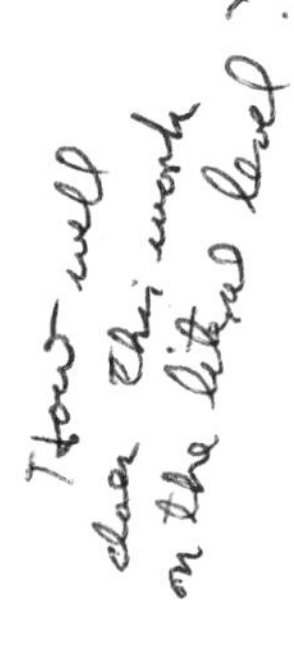

On Sunday afternoons the girls
in their thin silk dresses walk out lithe
bellies swaying bottoms swinging
while pince-nez pigeons creak aside
pretending with a superb
unnoticed condescension no acquaintance
but the old benched men
sifting the ashes of yesterday's
newspapers sense behind their eyeballs
distant burning
signals of countries long unvisited
and sailors
stealthily detach themselves from chewing gum
and start the stalk and all the leaves
are green again.

BIRD IN HAND

The way the poet eats the hard-boiled egg
is this: he first chips delicately all round
the thin resistance of the shell of fact
which falls like flakes (if alabaster
melted so it would before
his beaming eye) as flicked
by his dactylic finger, to reveal
the gleaming nacreous shape
like a monstrous pearl—
he bites, good appetite, the simile in two
and sinks his teeth in muse's pollen,
golden, dusty, the real thing
that might once spring a phoenix to confound
the ovoid gape of his astonied stare.

MISS DICKINSON

She cut the wrapping paper neatly
into rectangles—no one would ask why,
it was New England's way—you saved
against the day. No matter what

the parcel had contained,
butcher's delivery, book
by some downstate sage, immediate
scissors flamed in her pocket.

New England makes its women
strange now and then—they take
to cats, or murder, often
in multiples; but she,

compound of thrift and greed
in primstitched white, preferred
to catechize mortality
in the side yard, and afterward

scratched on what leaves
(maple, perhaps, or elm)
only an oracle of Amherst,
Massachusetts, could command

the gist of the matter. Thrift
may have special uses—
likely the household's
other women saved the string.

THE RIDE

The white hair of the old
lady in the closed
window of the black
automobile. She sits
very straight, looking from right
to left as the car
turns the corner.
She is being taken for a ride, is it
by her son or perhaps a dutiful
middle-aged nephew.
The trees drop a few leaves in token.

Ach, the white
cotton wool
and the two grasshopper eyes
peering on stalks this way
and that.
She is helpless, she is old.
I do not want to be like that
taken for a ride by Mr. I-Don't-Know.
Keep your leaves, trees, don't write to me.

COMING HOME

I leave my armor by the umbrella stand and enter.
  At the first word I think of stone
    walls, sea meadows, and the sweet
      fearful smiles of old ladies in streetcars.

Blood of my blood and bone of my bone
they sit and stare me down.
His hands with tender spots of age
spread like soft meat on either knee.
"The hollyhocks this year–the salt air
brightens them, y' know. (Had you forgotten?)
What d' you have out there–
linden, is it? Immigrant shrub."
Her fingers clasp each other in the lap
where once, unborn, I must have leapt
half symbol, half embarrassment.
"We were a little disappointed–" she begins
with terrible timidity.
Love trembles in the proffered cup.
Then seedling, shifting, swelling,
sprouting, flourishing, brandishing, shaking-
shouting tree of pride, fruits pumice-
textured, clustered, shrunken,
color of never and despair–
                                        but after all,
what have they done to me, what crime
committed time on time in this small room?
And my own children, yet to be?
Splay-fingered, milky-mouthed, they will of course
love me, love me, love me.

CONCENTRATION

Goody-Goody's
thrown on the fire
there she goes
there she is

shovel of ash

Her little toenails
like blackened rose petals

Here is her hatpin
here is her buttonhook
here is her gold tooth
It is a game of objects that we play

MARTHA SONG

I go about my house with a dustcloth every blessed
morning.
Sweep and vac
front to back

shake the mop from upstairs windows
wipe the sills and polish dead
curves of furniture.

What the table what the chair
don't say when I'm not there
I'm sure

I should care. I shine china plates like smiles.
My house gleams
like a shell.

If I remember, if I have the time
I might carry water outside to the dying

flowers I planted in baked cracked earth.
Christ!

Too obvious an effect?

BELDAM

Now that I'm certified,
now I'm insane,
I don't have to come in
out of the rain,

I wear the cap and bells,
I bear the drums,
and I won't tell you
when the bogeyman comes.

I go by children
I hold my breath
so it won't fall on,
pearl them with death.

Abba, I nibble on water,
Abba, I moon on air.
Later, I'll show you the mousehole
under the tilted stair.

ON THE POSSIBLE KILLING OF A THREE-MONTHS CHILD BY A RABBIT

Was it raining, did the street lights bleed
rosy haloes through the city mist?
The weather might be important. / But then again - -
Was it a beautiful night?
Oh, the red eyes, oh, the vibrissa
hanging over the raddled couch.
And the fur, like cotton candy, like the ghost of the biggest
snowman.
Where did it grow, how did it get itself
out of the cage, out of the newspapers?
It was someone's pet, for God's sake?
WHO WAS THE FRIEND?
The father snores.
I knew a lady once pulled out
her eyelashes by the roots.
She was tall as a poplar,
pale as an ash.
Did the flesh
taste sweet, like new lettuce leaves,
wild onions, milky as white rose petals?
From the little stump a rubbery string
drools like the shred
of a red balloon. Sleep, baby.

TRANSFERENCES

This is my year for looking
ironically beautiful.
People respond to me.
What big eyes I have!

They are glass.
Such glossy hair,
it is made of damp chestnut leaves.

My skin has the fashionable
pallor of arsenic.
And that fine-boned nose!
Precisely.

Ego is a malodorous weed.
Such long nails!

FEVER

I take it my real child is ill.
The worm works in the rose, and fever
glisters in tower windows.
Can my thorn draw her poison?
Extreme caution must be exercised.
I must exercise extreme caution.
My medicine is very powerful.
It has already killed several.
I stand at the foot of her white bed
and tell her of her pet toad
whom she has named Mortimer, after
a friend of the family. I say that Mortimer,
patient, self-effacing, utterly reliable,
waits for her under the laurel hedge.
Her eyes are so bright!
Outside, the rain falls like fat gray slugs.

YEAR-ROUND

With what deceptive
gradualness the summer guests
depart,
bearing the various trophies
of their stay, shells, driftwood
antlers, a seabird's skull,
leaving
for our instruction shards
of the season's visit: sand on the stairs,
odd sneakers, a torn sweater, a child's ball,
and on the dressing table an unmailed letter.

One afternoon the last car disappears.
The hand raised in farewell
flags, drops. We linger
a moment at the edge of lawn,
knowing that soon we must go in,
desert the view, diminish
scene. Bring in the chairs
from the terrace, store the picnic things,
cover the boat. The house will need repairs—
look, that shutter
flaps.

Only, the clock
gnaws in the hall
like a mouse in the rind
of yellow time.
Let us make tea, learn chess,
revive the art
of conversation; read; take naps.
A toothless sea
mumbles at the crusts of the land.

AFTER THE STRAVINSKY CONCERT

i

Introduzione:

voce
principale

One day the pier glass in the entrance hall
swayed slightly, shuddered, and slid down the wall.
Just so an aunt of mine
was found once, sitting on the parquetry
in the same place near dawn, her wreath awry
and roses on her breath; but that perhaps
is neither here nor there, the glass uniting both
having long since been carried to the lumber-room,
leaving us nothing to reflect upon.
The gilded frame
was loosened and the mirror cracked. A cherub lost
a flying ribbon and whatever
had been underneath was only plaster.

ii

Larghetto indeciso:

vocina

Fell of its own weight was the verdict I knew better
girl though I was then, not yet risen
from the kitchen where that afternoon
the dishes rattled like the bowels
of a starving man they said along the gallery
the pictures swung as if freshly hanged
and in the drawing-room the vases chattered
like nervous women in a thunderstorm—
it was the boys
old men now stuffed with honors till their eyes
bulge out as if already marble
noble this and noble that on Sundays
glossy in the sups you might have seen
my photo too last birthday toothless I looked
but at least alive—I was saying
the nephews jumping on the beds upstairs
that was the cause. Your grandmother
was fond of them Lord alone knows why fond-
foolish if you ask me or else proud

to be bewildered so.
They should never have been invited at all.

iii

Andante sostenuto:

voce principale

Not half an hour before the fall, my grandmother
had stood impaling with the perfect calm
of confidence in time and place her floating hat
upon a pin; perfectly gentle, perfectly good,
pierced thus the instant, crowned herself
innocent patroness of place and time.
This was her afternoon to call.
The mirror gave her back her face
wondrously like: she knew
exactly where she was within the frame,
could lift a gloved finger if she wished
to touch the earlobe where the pearldrop sprung
chaste fruit of gold, and what she saw
she touched could feel, by sense and reason
mirror-assured that touch and sight were one,
aspects of distance and the moment joined
in a grave image of reality, as if she had been swan
and glass the stilled
water she moved on, making a single silvered self
(liable, however, to current and the wind
shaking the silvered surface of the dream).
When she came home, here the great boys had been
and had their game. She did not scold; said merely
she had been fond of it; had it put away.
The frame, she said, might someday be of use.

iv

Scherzo, mancando poco a poco:

voce principale

The house stayed wide, the gardens blowing
garlands of light and roses through the open doors,
the lawns with blandly insolent grace unrolled
in green chiaroscuro to the little lake
below the pavilion where the spoilt peacocks screamed
for tidbits from the luncheon guests who strolled
in clothes appropriate to the view.
Beyond, the ground-flowers in the meadows fairly

hiccupped out of the grass, and the gilt-edged sun
beat like a gong about the rooks all summer long
wheeling and wheeling in the burnished sky.
We never saw it that way.
Something had altered by the time we came,
something we could not put a finger on
but felt insensibly the absence of
had been withdrawn; some force which would surround,
protect, make fast a floating present; stay
the nettle and keep out the rot.
The place seemed at loose ends.
When we first found the pier-glass in the lumber-room
we were amused a while to see how true
had cracked so easily to false, or, it might be,
from false to true; and minced and mimed,
though Reba, the youngest, held up, cried:
her nose was flawed like her old doll's.
The game queered, we slammed outside.
The sky was threatening somehow; had crazed,
turned tarnished, and at the last
let down its brittle rain.
We sat against the wall and watched
the season going under in the fall.

V

Finale:
grave assai:

This is November of no beggars riding,
no more strawberries and cream, when Babylon
is gone out with the candle and the seam

coro

is none too fine. Night descends early now,
it's hard to tell the substance by these shadows.
The thin wind blows hey moaney o,
fragments and shards! fragments and shards!
No nonnies, no nannies, no go, lovely rose.
We sit against the wall and stare
into the splintering of air.

REVENANT

i

The day my father died in burning fall,
pyres were lit all up and down the streets;
and on the afternoon I saw his recent ghost
it came—no more a Lucifer
than any other man's or Faustus either—
it came, again I say, upon the haze
hung like a summer's cerements
thick and sententious in the anxious air.
But he came quick, familiar glint
of calmly humorous inquiry
a nick in the corner of his eye.
Windows were open, I was playing
unaccustomed Chopin in the mist
that smoked the mirror, made the cat cough
and curled the fern's fingers back towards dust.
Had I been playing Bach
I doubt my father would have come,
for, as it happened, he had only one
piece to his name,
almost the slowest Prelude in the book,
single survivor of surly Saturday mornings
chopped into little pieces by the clock
while in his brain the spit-lovely, curving ball
arced purely, maddeningly, through seraphic blue.

ii

Surely the teacher stayed, let alone returned,
solely because of my grandmother's coffee,
deep, strong, and bitterly bracing,
support, so she claimed, for the silver spoon
dipped by the innocent into the red-gold brew
this clattering tall witch brought with the steam

still on it, fresh from her chivvying.
The boy slipped out and ran towards his own way.
I knew the parlor well, from childhood summers on.
Cool, high-ceilinged, rosewood, mahogany,
words over memory like a chime: here shall they sit,
be summoned up and wound, submit once more,
the foreign, patient master with his awkward shoes
primly together under the dark plush pall,
the talking woman with her full blue eyes
flashing out kindness as it were argument.
The table between them's firm as the equator.
Beside these curios, those in the what-not dim
(even the giant conch, borne back a trophy,
pink as a god's other ear, from Atlantic City
and my grandparents' wedding trip).
She lets him off
before he grows too weary, but she does not fail
to note the exhaustion of his drooping cuffs.
It does not matter that I never saw him.
He wore a pince-nez, parted his thin gray hair
in the center, had a trick
of pressing his finger-ends as though in prayer;
lived in one room above the post office,
had no piano, practised at the church;
cared overmuch for beauty considering
his means and his existence; died
weightless, smiling ambiguously, and left no will.
And yet my father learned his piece.

iii

Ontario springs are rain-flogged out of winter's
chilblained grip. Ice boomed
and buckled on the Chippewa, the puck
skidded, striking rime in sprays; girls screamed,
scarves streaming red like February dawns,
as the whip snapped and skirts went flying
showing a tingling glimpse of wrinkled cotton shins.
By late March the ice was used up, yellow,
and willows took the yellow towards their green.

You had to watch the rotted wooden sidewalks
as, burbling with tonic, challenging the cracks,
you swaggered out adolescent as the season.
From the veranda, Emma and Maud waved Saturday
dustcloths and shouted something rude.

They were the older sisters, Allegra next,
Bertha the baby. My father was nearly christened Paul,
indeed was called so for his first few months,
but my grandmother changed her mind the week before
the ceremony; she had no time to read
except while nursing, and that year
it was Goethe (in translation), so it was John
anglicized and wailing in his lace-trimmed robe
who was sprinkled the only son instead.

My grandfather was in groceries,
natural gas, washing machines, lord knows,–
a Personage with a capital,
the cock of his hat, the lilt of his moustache,
the heft of chain across his vest told that.
Raised in the midst of presbyters,
he backslid gradually from divvying
the children with his Anglican
on alternate Sundays to the porch
hammock and counting ruby-throated
hummingbirds while, very black-and-white,
very erect, she set out trailing charges
like a swift silken kite. "Fifty-six
at service," she would report, and he
respond, "Eleven at the trumpet vine."

One day they take the boat to Buffalo,
he has a man to see; she has the stores,
of course, and asks no questions, being here,
and only here, diffident. They arrange to meet
at 2 p.m. at a monument they both like.
She is there. She is there a good hour,
grown very tall, moreover, and beset
by pigeons. "Tommy," she says in a voice
of thinnest glass, "where have you been?"
with Sir Harry Oakes in his private plane.

"I've been flying," says Grandfather, "all over Buffalo
He found it was my birthday." And settles his chin
onto his collar with absolute éclat.
He took five teaspoonsful of sugar in his milk,
but it was Russian rubles did him in at last.

His mother lived along another street.
John was her favorite. A little boy
in knickers with a devilish bright eye
he stood behind her chair in hottest June
and fanned her heaving, purple chest.
Immensely old, immensely fat, she fought
the ostrich feathers with her jagged breath
and wheezed against her fancied ills,
slightings by relatives, stealing by kitchen girls,
asthmatic whispers coiling in his ear
like the fierce distant thunder in a shell.
Still he was fascinated, even when
as it were between complaints she gave a sudden gasp,
clutched at eluding air, and went right under.
It was the silence, not her final glare,
fixed and affronted, freed his howl
and flung the fan down at her slippered feet
and sent him thudding home to beggar noise.
The following week he drowned
Allegra's coral brooch in the sulphur well
and was soundly strapped. His sobs
were loud with gratitude.
Was taught to swim by being rowed
to the river's middle, harnessed to a rope
and tossed in; down he sank
thrashing like any sunny into the rank
muddy whorls, and rose up gagging
for his pa's laughing under his panama;
his father hauled him in hand over hand,
tossed him again, again; until
the boy glistened and panted like a tadpole
and took the other element for pleasure granted.
The sun was staggering on the western slope
when the pronouncement came: "Now you can swim,"
the tamer said, and lit a fresh cigar.
The boy never doubted it was true.

One wet, one dry, they headed for the shore
where Emma flapped the supper semaphore.

iv

A gloss of days: one guesses, one must guess.
In the upstairs hall there hung a length of frame
entitled *Life's High Moments*. After the bassinet,
hooded like a snuffer, and the child
velvet-suited, banged, and guarded by
the Saint Bernard whose tongue lolled sweetly out,
a young gentleman in faultless evening clothes
correctly bowed before a maiden piled with hair.
The next panel showed the wedding, she
impenetrably veiled, and after that
they got into the carriage and were driven off.
And then? And then? We do not know.
We are not apprised. We imagine gone
what we are not sure existed even once—
school fights, bad dreams, the poster pointing
you to fight the Huns: the night the horse was tied
to the banister on the second floor
of Croyden House; free-lance experiments
in foggy fields, knowledge the premised province—
it receded, rather. . . . And all this, all these
gone by and hardly reconciled
with what has come, and been, and gone again.
I enter late,
with other burdens, into smaller rooms.
The dimpled moon that drew you by her smile
into her sphere outlasted you
and now sinks sidewise with her numbing grin
hugely enspreading whatever face you loved.
Can I restore you to a simpler tune
than that which wrangled out our times that mingled
making the players fret and mumble too?
It is dusk now. Do not light the lamp.
Let the place be neutral, somewhere between
my haunted present and your haunting pale.
Peace to the footfall, rapid and sentient;
let be resolved and recognized lost seasons; wait
for the steady, lifeless breathing of the snow.

THE HERON

i

What does he make of it all,
the solitary blue
heron standing unmoved
and motionless these hours
on the most delicate
elongated leg like black-
lacquered bamboo in the shallows
at the far end of beach beyond
the weedy place where the shore curves
in, against the lake and sky,
and darker and stiller than each?
It is the smaller blue,

not like yet something like
gulls of my childhood, summer's
easy skimmers (how we entered leaping
into the arched hollow murmuring mornings),
divers and swimmers of the foam and air
whose sun warmed the numbed rocks and rose
to be cooled the whole day in the sea,—
stung into alabaster motion by the salt-
spray rush and flash of the glittering roll,
the hugely tremulous coruscating infinite-seeming bolt of blue
drawn out to crash or crawl, to curl along or cover
the lift and sprawl of coast, granite and sands
(we castled, pooled at the water's edge,
and heaped on laughing, quivering-limbed
companion corpses with their heads stuck out
and eyes shut dry on imitation dark,
the resurrection always
miraculously quick, the gritty ritual play of child-
death washed off in the instant's
plunge, the race back
with droplets scattering from our heels, and the gulls'
cries about us like new
flakes of light); free-
wheeling runners of the deep between sky and ocean,

released by season's change from slow-
sailing vessels of dull pewter flight
against the wrinkled slate or purple sullen heave,
or points
of wintry meditation fixed
like puritan heads on pilings sheeted green
with freezing slime for Sunday parents to hold up
to muffled (younger) thumbwise child
sucking with vaporous eyes no more than naughtiness
rewarded in less lenient, February age,–
or was there caught perhaps a latent strange
rich breath from suffering's hoary marshes?–

turned again
transformed forms, their white calls
garlanding granite lovers convolute at noon
in the rude crannied shelter of the rocks'
embrace, come onto just before the jump
in the game's metamorphosis, the circus act
of vaulting miles of lions' backs
humped passive to the flying foot
on their pocked tawny hides: the forced
flailing stop, stumble, tamer spun away
shouting into the spume flung to corroborate
betrayal of beasts thought safe,

and falling, like petals, like wafers dissolving
in the heat's blaze and shimmer, off into gradual silent
sounding while their wings' white phrases
rent in articulating space
wavering,
winding, mending itself without a flaw
over the darkening sea-flayed cliffs, the swaying
sea-buoyed bells off Ninigret,
Sachuest, Quonochontaug and up the bay
to Galilee, Jerusalem on the other side,
chanting in frail monotonous voices borne
on the creaking wind of chasms and islands underneath.

ii

Such paraphernalia trailing,
having already the sight in passing

this morning of the farm wife
crossing the yard to set the fresh-filled basin
for the more timid birds under the mallows hedge,
and a corn-color sun
flowered round as a gold watch in the dome
of a county sky showing fair above the dawn
clouds fraying at the eastern rim, we came
over the slight rise planted in coarse grass
to keep the slope from blowing, this brown sand
grainy as burlap to bare soles. No matter:
there was the lake, and the children streaked
forward to make the first assault on the calm
stretch of tawny beach
like the dozing farm dog one steps over in the entry
almost unnoticing, on the way outdoors
to assume the day
with a flurry of shrieks and splashing, waking the water,
pricking the inland balsam air they know
their shrillness zig-zag echoing
off the bluffs opposite, but the lake
in its level saucer did not tilt even a little bit.
If the heron was here then we did not see him.

iii

Did cocks prepared to split the husk of night
sense alien wing oar steady past the red-
roofed farms and silos sleeping upright
through the dark moving wedge translating dark,
and hesitate so that the sun for once
eluded gaping beaks and sprang
unspurred while doubt turned momentary heads
towards westward wake till memory
or something like for water, reeds,
and a sky caught in a rippled net had curved
him to touch down upon the bordering trees
and shake off flight amid a hood of leaves?

iv

Not till near ten o'clock it must have been,
but out here we are

at least an hour behind, and the day
behind that in summer, so must one go
by appearances, time
out of mind: let us just say

it was after the apparition of the small green boat
from the cove on the lake's further side,
like a pod slid on silk, with the three
figures, faceless, brimmed to scant the glare
and yet delivered by it to a larger sphere,
dowered by mists drawn off, to the shore
watcher shown as they were and something more,
presiders, harbingers, of this clime and that,
ample in faded milkish blue, august in azure paled,
their playing lines like fated threads
to gather up the water-marked
puckered seam of their going, themselves
unmoving, without speech, without haste or lingering
across the middle distance to the reach
of the land's narrow arm escaped,
and glided out of grasp and view of the exterior eye
shuttering to an interval's
suspense like the faint humming of a shell

or a wire rubbed to singing; but not before
the boy and girl made sure of, bobbing oblivious,
and, in the lower corner of the scene,
the shadow sensed of foreign shape or signature
to the event; opening on what old

(parliaments of bent, burnished women
having removed their shoes as for a ceremony
at the tide's turn hauling their flimsy chairs—
wrested from tenement top porches strung with soot-
stippled washing, pickets out
like brawled teeth, staggered by bawling children
obscurely envied from the car
on the short cut home to the cleanly haloing
flame for the kettle and the neuter egg
in the scalded china cup,
with antiseptic lilacs peopling the window screen
above the flat scrubbed table after the Sunday ride
to avoid the indiscriminate humidity—
right into the water for the last look and gossip

while at their feet the new colonial
babies dabbled and tumbled in the rosy foam
and frowning mothers stood in rows, transplanted
caryatids talking of Caesareans by a sea
that was the same yet not the same
as in the former center of the world
now shifted to mere seething in the blood
on pavement Saturday nights in the absence
of eagles for processions; but the old ones sighed
perhaps, hearing the indefatigable gulls scream in
the fishing fleet from a foundered sun)

things wondered at and wound on what loose skein
to brush the thin eyelid of the present
that it interprets instances as signs
or hieroglyphs as presences translating an entire
past into a single form imbued
with color and endowed with breath,

the heron had come forward,
sundering
vines hung charm-like on the doorway
of the cell in the overhanging
wood where light ran tremulous
and vague among tangled roots;
entering
with a soft plosion of elated blue
onto the riffled air, into the clear,
and then the sudden braking by intent
or chance, and the unerring riding down
the invisible flume to the strand,–

but this imagined: what was awaked
aware to was the opaque
countering
by stillness as would not occur
to stone but rather in the pine branch
strict and plumaged, balancing
fluidity and brilliance that would whelm,
blind, drown and drain dry, by a weight
of feathers stitched to finest bone, the oblique
answering
to earlier signal quilled in water,
while the children sharply cried their Look!

v

Look! What did his eye,
what does his eye take in
now morning has been swung to afternoon
and we are joined by others of our kind,
now garbled picnics have been spread
and trampled after the Sunday School mass
hazing of the spirit so it thirsts
inordinate for sweet drinks labeled pure
and fresh immersion christens earth's salt innocents?
For still he stands,
not put off by the crowd
or voices multiplying flat syllabic caws
to cause an agitation of the day's sequences
so that the ordering is changed upon the scrim
of intimation as it hangs, gauzy with heat,
before us and we gaze bemused
through drowsy meshes now perturbed
as by insects caucusing above the churned
tepidity towards which he inclines
alert, attentive, strangely courteous
and remote; the grasses trembling slightly
always about him on the littoral. He too must see

how farmers when they get in boats make furrows
out of habit, mariners of the plow,
grins scarring weather-stiffened flesh
at unaccustomed gunwale
antics of their squealing young,
or, at the barrier, how couples with hasped arms
are treading living thigh to thigh,
trading glazed stares and laved
by liquid substitutes, their commerce
languid and the yield foregone; must be
observer of the anxious promenade
of the perpetual second cousin plump and pale
as a puffball, proud no doubt
of her small feet and supple bangled wrists
that tap and toss out vined veranda tunes
on heavy evenings after the faint din-
dunning declension of some dead saint's bells,—
who rigged now in tropic rayon and pink gloves

alarms herself for her dog's sake that the boys
are throwing sand again; again, scans where
shorn of their voyages, shades in the sun
they pushed all day across the prairies,
ravishers of sod and shy of women,
the old men dangling loose in clothes
having more wear than they can use,
the somehow puritan ardor in their veins
turned now to ichor subject to the cold,
watch as from lichened agates how things are
without them as they were, converse
from mossy caverns, hollowly,
halting hawk and spit
rehearsing how the freezing hiss of rheumy rain
plagues the interstices of wind-kilned bones.
But at the first frill of the fretted lake
a child steps and cavorts with a red parasol,
practising earliest deceits and favors
with rosy lady's battered little shadow,
gayest ruins streaming silken ribbons rivulets.

vi

What shall be made, what shall I make of that? I
who in human guise hover and marvel, spy
and adorer, ruthless pardoner, and find
my mind's eye swells and boggles at such troves,
desiring to embrace the entire, may fail and fall
utterly into my own swift fallacies,
mistaking sight for vision and the naming
for the possession of, likewise the past
for my own simple history (I would not wish
a simple history for anyone),
and either praise too much
or rail how we are islanded in time,
pilgrims and immigrants from a world
we never knew, left languageless,
bereft and half-blind on a rock,
a mere pimple in a vast waste of surly roil,
and turn to picking over bits of broken shell
such as are dropped from indifferent beaks
to smash on granite a sea mile below,—

stooping, we gather up such treasures
slowly, slowly, under the decaying day,
later to lap and mumble in the clammy chambers
who has the most, the prettiest, the best,
and when the night is darker we will murder him,
he having amassed attempted beauty out of litter
and thus a kind of speech and this a crime,—

so fancy runs and blinks and feeds upon the scene
the same yet not the same another eye
assesses opposite: the pinpoint eye,
the glistening black seed of vision, tiny orb
that makes the universe an exercise in minimals,
going back, beyond myth, beyond malignant or benign
interference with earth's dust
molding and naming parts of man,
beyond disappointment then, or shame,
to scale us with the primary essences
we carry in us, equal in value to the pile of sand
before which the boy and girl kneel in attitudes
of curious homage; allowing therefore the return
towards evening to the emptying beach
of actual country women in a small green boat,
a little tired may be and thinking of chores
waiting, and husbands, and certain wicks to trim:
letting them be miraculously what they are.
What do you answer here, my heron? Phoenix
of place, prophetic bird, time's arbiter,
the heron keeps his distance still; and always will.
Voices come flute-like at this hour on the pellucid air.

CONVERSATION: LATE DAY

What was so bright is fading now. Is it not
fading? The sun slants
oddly. *Differently, that's all.*
The paper's peeling roses in the hall.
The boarders use the phone too much, and scratch
their numbers on the wall. I'll move the bench.
But Mr. Quinquagesima will fall
off; he's dead, remember, these two years.
Oh, surely more.
I've given out directions to the girl
to dust around him. I don't want
him disappearing in a cloud like What's-his-name.

Watch your step,
that brick is crumbling there.
Which frets me. As you know, I don't like change
however small; if this goes on,
earth will be nibbling at my toes.
I could find someone to repair it,
I daresay; I'll ask tomorrow. Don't,
don't speak the word! No, leave it,
since we must learn to give
in, I suppose, to these natural
processes. I sigh; but then to show
I bear no grudge, you may
cut off some heads for me. Over this way,
and with your military cane take care
of that frowziness. I find chrysanthemums
unsatisfactory except as wigs
to scatter thus like pale rinds on the grass.
Grass! It's hay. Where is the boy
who used to come here? Oh, he changed–
changed greatly. . . . Give me your arm:
how firm it is, like a young man's still.

No one would dream
it's sawdust underneath your clothes.
Where is the boy? I beg

you, don't go on
in that direction, you will only
upset yourself. Remember,
we are walking in the garden, and the day
is surely stopped at four o'clock
just as it should be. Is it not?
That shadow has not moved, it has not moved?
I am afraid that sometimes I may sleep
or grow to drowsiness or is it wake?
I know there's something between day and morning
for, though you may laugh, I've felt it there,
a shape between us, not what you may think
but a gray mass, amorphous, breathing
(holding of breath is part of breathing),
biding its time—it's time I hate,
I'll take no notice of it, hear?
Hush, the boarders. One,
the fat girl in pink frosting, hangs
her stockings from the upstairs balcony.
That's only Flossie, of the thick
ankles and thicker mind. *Are you quite fair*?

It's Mrs. Quinquagesima I fear:
she's always praying, on her knees
on the scabby linoleum of her room,
as though through them some transcendental
whisper may yet come. Why does she leave
her door open? When I pass
she's spitting in her palms. Prayer
makes me uneasy. *Incense is bound*
to fester in this air; would it divert you
if we took another turn, as far, say,
as the firebush, or perhaps
the boneyard? Yes, that dog
is getting beyond himself. The pile
sprouts like the tusks of old
potatoes, and I see
the tatting on the roof
of the house is ravelling, but then
tatting's susceptible to weather.
Can't you arrange it so one season
will include all? *As it was I had to touch*
the capital, I had to vouch to keep

these gobblers of your grandmother's preserves!
The cellar's deep, the shelves hold what we need.
Remember other suppers waiting, clean
new-laid eggs, rice-chicken-fish on the checkered
cloth; the cook impatient (servants always are)?
But it was summer then. . . . You have distracted me:
where is the sun
now? Terror, I feel terror.
My shawl, hand me my shawl, the chill
will shake me open so I'll spill
like birdseed. *Close your eyes, you must*
close your eyes to hoard the light
from day to morning. Was that bells
beyond the wall, or only thunder?
My hair smells sulphurous. *Come in,*
my dearest love, and close your eyes.
Your chatter maddens me. *I meant*
to comfort you. You meant, you meant
it's I who means, you're simply cursed
with what I mean and what I've had to do.
Don't dwell on it. Hurry, come in,

I tell you the bush is blackening.
The sky is washed with yellow. How the trees swell,
as though they'd crack like knuckles.
Will you come? Yes, yes, yes, yes,
you are right. We must look
alive.

THE GATHERING

i

Evening: At Table

I have remembered sense of generations
packing in close about a feast of time
as though existence were a dining table,
we the invited guests, and I a child again
and pressed between the two tall bony aunts
whose silk skirts spill along my skinny shanks,
whose heads like weedy flowers nod
emphatically across me on their stems
showing the stringy tautened cords
attaching them to Sundays such as these.

Summer. Evening. The dark-veined honeycomb
of glass, the colored dome to childish eyes
a marvel is slid downward on its chain
and sheds its colors as it comes
to harlequin us all. Features stand out
suddenly: an older uncle will begin to look
like his own mother as she looked in age;
his wife will give her maiden name away
in her hand's shape, as if a common line
were written in her palm,–
a dozen like it gesture down the row.
Light falls upon a cheek as it did years
ago for someone else,
and little Shelagh's got the double crown.
We pass our plates up for the victuals,
talking the whole time, or the grown people do,–
interspersed others clutch soft silver spoons
teethed over long since by their elders;
eager in bibs, and propped, they lean
forward and breathe, and slobber slightly,
dazed by the noise, the smells, the light.
(A missing few went earlier to bed,
netted about in hasty cots to listen to

the last birds meting out a day
so brief it must have seemed the sun
opened its eye once fully, gazed gold, then
drowsed it closed again with theirs
and let the mottoes fade upon the wall
and vines and roses over them grow fast
in flowing dark, and cover up
their names.)
Outside, the moths beat furious at the window screen.
The lamp above us glows its blood-
red, blue, its brooding green;
but while the voices rise,
I see my mother sitting silent, pale,
skewered to pride and shyness by her cameo.

ii

Evening: The Mother

She sits stiff, crumbling bread, the smile
stretched tight upon her linen face.
Talk tires her, she often says.
Her rages are so private that they've bleached her gaze,
held lowered now lest it should show
dread or revulsion of the human tribe
she's been betrayed to. Oh, she is cold,
she cannot stand the draught
coiling round her shoulder. She is dry,
as though some spring were sealed from birth,
yet she can weep. She can weep.
Children she loves most when they sleep
or are ill; no one is then kinder,
gentler, more solicitous. Children when they sleep
must be covered; must not thrash; when ill
may be cared for tenderly; otherwise
must be punished gravely, else discover sin,
which will result in telling lies.
Stay still, she murmurs in her whitened tone,
lie down now; sleep. And goes a shade
of white out of the dusky room.

The child stares fearful into dark,
not knowing why. I will not know
till later what sleep means to her.

iii

Morning: The Grandmother

Long ago
this morning,
flattening myself
against my spine, I try
the top stair.
It makes no outcry, so I test
the next, and it receives me too.
The third step creaks
loudly; it makes a hole
in silence. I draw my foot back just in time
and wait, but the hall
above gives no sign; sleep
still holds them up there in a milky mist.
And I go on, picking my way,
my passage down
to seven o'clock of a fine
midsummer dawning past its rosy wake
and gone to flower within
the oriole window of the hall below.
I follow
clues: the cloudy cape
cowled on the newel post, daubed gloves
damp on silver tray, wet trail along parquet,
and chestnut-colored odor
curling beneath the kitchen door. Aha!
My father's mother, tall, hawk-
nosed and vigilant, has of course made the grand
first tour of the day.
Of the garden. In her man's
straw hat, and galoshes left
by some unremembered guest, and bearing
the flat wicker basket and the shears just as

sharp as mercy, she has visited
her stations; paused
to weed, to snip, to let in air about the roots;
and now, her apron on, the vases out,
poses at the counter, parrying
snapdragons!
Oh, it's you!
she says, and, Good: you can pit cherries.
But I don't know
how, I whine. She
shows me how my thumb can pop
the pit out neat as an eyeball. Charmed,
I set to work, we set to work.
"Juice makes a cherry," says the woman wisely,
sticking in stalks
pendent with bloom. "I wouldn't give a fig
for a cherry without juice."
We laugh easily together.
Shaping the day between us, our wrists run
with warmth, the quickness, the sweet light.

iv

Noon: The Grandfather

I am a lady now for solitude and green
wavering light at parlor French
long windows sunk in vines.
Armchair grandeur! Splendor of rose-
wood and mahogany, and don't forget
the faded Turkish carpet on the floor,
the mends don't show.
I pull a book whose leather flakes
like dried leaves from the shelf.
Happens it's Shakespeare, as I like it,
me, myself, some Rosalind
half-boy, all brave new world,
Miranda, root: to be wondered at, and lost
in profound reality, I reel a little, and read on.
"A dreadful light

to see by," says my prosperous
grandfather's voice from the doorway:
fingering the gold
chain across his vest, he makes his choice,
advances to the piano stool, and sits,
knee cocked jaunty over
other, Sabbath trouser leg. Oh, the swell
his prideful belly makes in person and in place.
You'd think he embodied half the globe.
I do not quarrel with that. I admire
his black magic broadcloth and his milkweed hair.
He smells of Yardley's, wears a boutonniere,
he counts
his children's children like his dividends.
He describes a half turn on his axis,
shoots his cuffs and flexes
manicured fingers over the yellowed keys,
that tumble to his touch like dominoes.
Shower of notes, pattern of ivory tune
woven into leaves that tremble each
a listening, veined, lady's lobe to tease.
"D' you know
what tune that is?" he asks, not stopping
playing, and I hazard Sunday-wise,
"A hymn?" He chuckles. "Not a bit of it.
'Old Black Joe,' with variations. . . . Ha!"
Not stopping yet, but softer, "Had a colored
handyman once, name of Teller. Simple-
minded, but a wizard with the hoe.
Teller confused me with God. Got so
your grandmother called me that to him.
'God wants the radishes thinned. God wants
the bay hitched up, He has to see a man.'
One day the tool shed caught fire. Teller yelled.
'Get God and send a bucket!' Shack gutted.
Teller only said God moved too slow."
"And did she ever call you God after that?"
Diminuendo and amused, "You know,"
he says, "she never did."
And musing, slows, bemused,
stops. "Perhaps that was just as well."
His smile is not for me. "It is the cause,
my soul. . . .' What was his wife's

name? Daisy. Yes." Light and quick shadow play
across his face. The tall black clock lets fall
eleven wafers into the crack of time.

V

Noon, Afternoon: Relatives

Uncle Johnny comes just then,
dares to ask if that's too soon,
one eye blue and one eye brown,
hand out always, grin turned on,
plunks him down and starts to croon
how his wife has left again.
How I love my uncle John.

Twin
ancients, sisters in their skin
and bone
of bone, but somehow
fleshless in their scrawn,
sit side by side in lady
chairs and bleed disdain.
High thoughts have drawn their tempers thin.
Dried lips are formed to speak
a no, or yawn.
They have forgot, if ever they have known,
how seldom is a goose mistook for swan.
Is there no beauty here? Yes, in she comes,
bearing the rosy garland of her afternoon
that has not yet begun to wane;
pranced after by her two young blooms,
two variants of a single stem
so smooth, so slender as to seem
new-sprung, although the lines
like light thorn-marks have, in the light,
begun to show beneath those beaming eyes
that shed light like twin prodigals of love.
Her husband walks a pace behind
"Father!" she says, and stoops
to conquer that old bastion with a kiss,

"Now, Eva," he says, skittish, pleased.
"I saw you only yesterday."
And pats her bottom as a fond papa will.
Her husband glares.
He cannot help it that he looks so pale,
as if he lives forever in the shade.

I look at her, and she is like a swan.

vi

Night: At Table

I float on swirling waters, laughter, voices,
I twirl a silver spoon.
My eyes burn, my head throbs with heat and noise,
but that's all right.
But all the faces look alike,
I hear a tune that runs along my brain,
it recapitulates itself and runs a-new.
It turns me in the whirlpool of a yawn.
And, "Time to go!" My father's voice. He
gathers me, almost hauls me up and away
from light, from the light, the rainbow-shed
blossoming, the giant flower that sways
above our table and our day and days.
"Good-night! Good-night!"

Later,
awake in the electric dark,
I hear the voices underneath the stars,
departing wheels, the calls, "Good-night!"
Footsteps on stealthy stairs.
And later still the faint click of slow heels
from outside, down on the portico
where the original hosts, arm in familiar arm,
pace like forgiving ghosts,
like the ghosts they will become.
Their guests have all gone home.
He throws away the end of his cigar,

How do you know?

and they go in. Gone home.
The house sighs once, and settles.
Out there, trees stir.
Sap rises in me, and I dream.

AFTERNOON OF A CONTEMPORARY POET

The friend who has a gall bladder
phones: the operation to be done
on Saturday. But only look—
the grand piano, suffering what indignities,
is rolling up the walk,
supported by three men. Crack crack
and crack the floor says, terrified.
"Do all floors do this in all houses
where you deliver pianos?"
"No, lady."
My son arrives from school, bearing a few
sad fallen leaves (it has rained since)
which we must enter immediately in
the dictionary. It is quite full already,
but he does not mind that. And out of these
will spin the tenuous free-wheeling web
of image, while from the top
of the refrigerator the Siamese,
vulture-like, brooding on fancied wrongs,
stares like the ultimate metaphor at five o'clock.

THE PERFECTIONIST

with apologies to John Crowe Ransom

She certainly died, though not
of the general human
fever. Of chills
which proved mortal she died,
and the rigor of pride.
In her vacuum she abhorred
Nature. Nature finally scored.
Her refrain:
"Choose. Reject.
Discard. Maintain.
The stars are false,
they've moved again."
See now the tall
and adamantine brow.
Beneath the lids
closed by the unsought mercy
of the living, eyes must be
still stonied by denial. Strict-
boned hands cling to
a wreath long withered.
Therefore in pity at least
let us bring a winter
garland spiky with unforgiving
green, darkly articulate,
the colder the weather
grows more defiant, and more beautiful.

AT MRS. R's

Breaking the surface of the long, umbrageous room,
rising as from the foam of some dry Venus-sea,
exquisite out of the Aubusson, the tea table:

bearing its rosy wreath of cakes and marzipan,
crested with silver urn perched and craftily jointed
like some heraldic creature wrapt from myth
and set to brood on china (Limoges) eggs.

One looks in vain for a mosaic eye.

The diffident sun, a poor relation
bidden at four, limps in pale vestments,
borrowed, down the andante gloom
peopled with cabinets and manners;
takes refuge finally in ambiguities
of shaded glass shielding too-soft breath
of calculated bloom.

Here pity is no more possible than beauty.

Meanwhile the alternate Thursday connoisseur,
approaching with tainted smile the hooded chair,
notes once again how authentic and how rare
the narrow anachronistic foot
suspended in its pliant, pointed case
of dull bronze leather at the end of the relique-
thin leg of her who is curator and core
of this unique collection opened to a select et cetera.

They say she sometimes sucks a ruby like a plum.

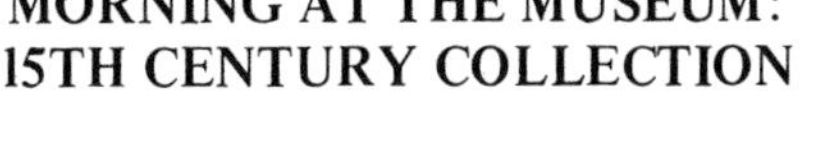

MORNING AT THE MUSEUM: 15TH CENTURY COLLECTION

Being a poet, naturally I was stirred
by such a frame of reference for love.
Now, as you pull on that soft, expensive glove

(which might have clothed some bestiary unicorn
fed in a garden on pears and cream,
brought up to nuzzle lady's fingers
and be rewarded by that same slow smile
a little inattentive as to a child not hers),

after the morning-full of madonnas
lapped with their haloed embryonic concepts
and all with the special blankness of the eye
showing intensity of spiritual concern
or else phlegmatic before such fruit and blossom
dangled as native to the slopes of Heaven:

after the triptychs spread like holy fans
or the stiff skirts of Flemish virgins
gravid with grace or secret self-possession:

after the landscape's vague suggestive spiraling
to the mere man-made tower or the tree
transformed somewhere along the corkscrew way
by the foreground domination of the maiden's head
turning them neutral on the cliffs of hills:

something of this and how you knot your scarf
of thinnest, most cerulean gauze
so that it frames your almost plumply oval face,
disturbing to the viewer in its calm
assumption of some prize I cannot even guess,
its inward-dwelling gaze, must give me pause.

"If they could speak," you murmured in the gallery,
"what would they say?"
Now your lips part again—
O, may the words fly forth each like a dove—

"Shall we have lunch?"
The blue ends softly fall in place. / of the scarf, first of all

A DREAM OF HEAVENLY LOVE AND REDEMPTION IN THE WOOD

Damn her whose image on my nightly eyes
Rises unbidden by my daytime brain,
Damn her, the false nun gliding black on snow
Within the winter wood to find my places out.
No shudder of stricken leaf foretells
Her coming where I cower amid thorns,
But all the birds sit frozen on the boughs.
Tall as a tower comes she down the ride,
Her train of sable fancies in attendance close;
From a sly fold of her dark habit, lies
Hang like a rosary to be told, or little bells
To cast a different death, to tell a different hour.
Her snouted hounds of Grace and Mercy run beside,
Fawning and leaping on their lengths of chain,
And all the birds sit frozen on the boughs.
Nearer they come, the ladies twittering, but she
Stopping them of a sudden with a hand
Raised as in supplication or surmise—
Mass in the thicket, compound of blood and fear,
Signal of tiny beating in the air, the pulse of red
Betraying the human trespass of the wood.
The dogs know now. Loosed at her nod, they do not bark
But come on silent as the trees,
No pause, no check, no circling back, but straight
To quarry, that stain on black and white,
And silent spring and before any cry
Can struggle from the beating throat
Beneath them, silently devour.
The softest clapping, as of snowflakes shaken from sleeves,
A smile as calm and faceless as the dark
Attend me on my waking into sleep,
And all the birds sit silent on the boughs.

MUSING IN NEW ENGLAND:
THE LONG LAST DAY OF MRS EDDICOMBE

". . . and stepping from thy Father's house harnessed a golden chariot, and the strong pinions of thy two swans fair and swift, whirring from heaven through mid-sky, have drawn thee towards the dark earth. . . ."

Sappho: "To Aphrodite"
translated by J. M. Edmonds

". . . Ah! when the ghost begins to quicken. . . ."

W. B. Yeats: "The Cold Heaven"

i

That morning opening
her eyes, cold from the sea-
damp night and seeing Day
again so clearly writ across the
curtains, Mrs. Eddicombe,
a lady of these parts, no longer young
(pluckings of dead
gray hair by dawn on the anxious pillow)
and never beautiful, however vain
(an arch of foot, a turn of wrist
were once admired; she married him
but kept the money in her name
had her two sons, and buried him,—
his actual services
were private, causing talk,
benched wit branched village-green
between hawk and spit
having it that he simply disappeared,
blew away, gone to seed at last
in that cliff-hanging garden up there, or,
wraith of a blithe
adventurer, lit out, West maybe,
past Albany: his stone,
stricken with gull-droppings, leans
anyhow in the churchyard, CAPTAIN
the granite legend reads, ay-uh)
speaks on a sudden out of dream-disordered sleep: "*Is it time*?"
Receives no answer, has expected none,

not knowing what it is she's asked,
and turns her face away from light.
Something she has been doing now for years.
Must struggle up, to stand upon the mat
and get her bearings. For the floor tilts.
And what old man
stares back at her from silt-encrusted glass?

ii

The slow stair rail unwinds
beneath her sliding palm. The landing window
gives upon the sea. If it is fine
weather, the sea is blue,
if not, the sea is gray.
The weather is fine today.
Mrs. Eddicombe is going down.
As she descends,
the sun through native bull's-eye
shoots such an arrow into her back!

That other witch has come.
She always comes
thank-God early, hobbling on her knobs,
bringing up with her village mist,
heaving the gate,
crushing the oyster shells to grit
(her husband beats her when he drinks,
red as a lobster claw). As to pearls,
pshaw! The rusted key
scrapes seven in the lock.
                                        In her cave
she slams pots, chips
blue enamel, works in steam,
issues to empty slops
over the cliff, or hang
the dishrag on the lilac bush.

While in the passage, needle's eye,
the mistress, having lost the thread,
searches along the verdigris-
stained wall for traces of a name.

She hooks her father's cloak
down from its peg that sticks
an admonitory finger out
through moss or mold,
and drapes its holey folds
about her bones. Endure,
endure! She has,
she will. Only, she feels the cold
more than she used to do, and the new
throbbing of a wound she thinks is old.

iii

The formality of walking down the path!
Toad under dock
leaf does not stir.
Why should he budge for this tall shade
that scarcely casts a breath?
Her spells have all run out.
He stays securely under warts
and hides his jewel. A critic's stratagem.
The garden seeds itself, and has this time.
A monstrous cabbage like a coarsened rose
blooms in the lily bed, defiant dreams
a king. Salt dreams. She makes her way
among the golden droppings of the sun,
the silver spittle of the snail.
To come to stone
set like a ruined throne at cliff's edge.
Here she sinks
down, fiddles with her fancy's mourning
thoughts, cedars grow close, and wild
birds coolly cry.

iv

Limpet-born to rock
of woman gone like foam
so soon she never was
remembered, that long time ago
a creature opened,
ignorant of whether eye

or mouth or genital,
but heard the ocean in her father's voice.
Ran free in meadows,
built on sand, went with the wind,
came in to cold, and winter's rheum.
Drank smoke from the chimney.
Somewhere in her father's cups
was introduced to rhyme.
Ah! Scribblings in the eaves,
her breath a freezing cloud
(like water struck from stone),
shadows of metaphors
hung soft as bats among the rafters.
Force brought her out with her
tell-tale finger.
Malevolence
sprung from a black umbrella
shook drops of warning in her father's face
and she found the burrs dragged from her hair
and herself in a tumbril
traveling at terrible speed
into exile, pelted
by mildewed gloves and the smell of pomade
and made to learn her catechism: female.
She never got used to that country.
She got out of it as quick as she could.
But some weakness clung,
and on top of that the old man died
of a brain swelling or a cracked heart
she imagined, and saw him unforgiven
sheeted on the tide.
High and dry
in the pale dune grass she spies upon
the young men
alien as earthly
gods with water-dropleted hair
and their girls in beach-head positions
drilling in the sandy hills.
Her body like a hollow shell. Will no-one come?
She swears she will make flutes
of all the blades within her bone-dry reach.
Will no-one come?
Foam sits the ocean like the ghosts of ghosts.

V

Her hand beats pitted stone.
She lifts her hand against the light
and gazes at it, wondering what leaf
it reminds her of, altered by air
to wafer flesh. It may fall, it may fall.
Her eyes fill, not with tears
but with ice. So many seasons
in one body! That has borne
the weight of bodies, nomad tenants,
hardly received, hardly nourished,
her fault, her flaw, her unnaturals.
Even her heat then was cold.
When her first was born
she moaned for a pencil.
The second was her favorite.
Till two he spoke no word, and then said,
"Light!"
At three he looked into her eyes
and said, "Black suns!"
She thinks now he was right,
and smiles a smile she does not know.
At five he gave up metaphor
and joined the other at his grub-dirt games.
She gave them up, and left off feeling warm.
Soon they all treated her like glass,
talking round her, through her, breathing rough
when she froze, but never splintered her,
just vanishing like early frost from pane.
The first bred earthworms in another part
of the country, but the second stayed
to invent a telescope that counted dust.
He had the attic room
till he was committed to a lower roost.
She cleared
his room out, sat her down
and wrote his death to life.
So it began,
or ended, the long
betrayal, the long withdrawal–she fell
onto words like spears,
pricked herself time on time like spindles.
She bled rose-red ice.

She in her tower,
and that other
in her cave. Their spells did not collide
but they were in cahoots all the same.
Collusion wound like spider's hair
around the moldings, up the stair.
It came and went like the sea-air
under doors. *Women, we are women here,*
it whispered. *We make monsters in dry wombs,*
out of the lime we blow from men's dead bones.
Outside, the ocean laughed and muttered in his beard.

vi

Did she sleep? Nod off
in the manner of the old?
It is already quite late.
Some wind forked like a snake's
cool tongue out of the pines
touches her through her shawl.
The sea below is purpling now,
shaking itself like the hem
of the dusk's garment. That is beautiful.
This stone is very hard.
She feels as if it holds her down,
as if she has been buried sitting up
and the earth turned inside out.
She has eaten nothing the whole day,
she could die here
for anyone's care! That is the way,
that is the way of the world.
The saddest phrase. She whimpers.
She must go in. Which way is home?
By the owl's cry, she cannot tell.
She stands. Lost, lost! The sun has gone,
the moon is brewing silver from the sea,
and who, and who will have the last word?
Under his leaf, the toad chuckles in his sleep.

vii

That night, she dreams.
She has been fetched out of dark,

brought back, fed like a child
at the kitchen table. Or was that
dreaming, too? She is sure
she cried and bit the spoon.
She is sure she is lying
in her bed, has long since
heard the shells' farewell,
the white wind
die. The sea asserts its hush,
hush. Curtains
bow once and retire. The night stands wide.
Is it mice gnawing she hears,
moss growing phosphorescent on the walls?
Old houses creak and sigh.
She cannot
uncross her hands from her withered breast.
A board, a bone snaps in the hall.
Light grows in dark if it is rotten.
This rot is dry, and light.
She feels her nails lengthen.
Her tongue stretches, labors: bursts.
A stroke of time, all arching anguish,
thrashing, come, she comes,
the most exquisite. . . .

viii

And love, words, love, her eyes
have startled into stone.
Father, forgive.

ix

Incantatory

Come again come
come all forbidden words
stars beauty flowers even love
put off disguises rise to me
press shells upon my eyes
that I may wake to night or dawn
but not this everlasting lidless nooning

breathe breathe rosy breathing lightly roar
against my parched ear that I may
not die as I have been here on my rock
exposed my tongue turned bitter root
that used to ripple out sound delicate with rime
into the time that had always something of morning
now who will comb
such kelped hair
like dried blood so it cannot hear
and such a dead
sea there dies daily hourly direly
oh I am drying in this sun
I watch the unveiled sky for a flight of swans

REVELATION

My grandfather once saw a black-
snake in the act
of swallowing a frog.
Quick as lightning Grandfather
fetched the axe,
smote that snake like thunder.
The frog sprang out and sprang away
across the meadow–likely to start
a new religion. Grandfather said
you never saw a frog
leap so high!

CEZANNE

The man astonished all of Paris
with an apple
but his wife
liked only Switzerland and lemonade.

HABITANT

Some people move about the world so easily
flying from the room that is
London to the lawn
of Vermont
to sit on whose terrace
when for an evening drink and exclaim
at which sunset
whereas
if I lived
in an attic with a cot
and a table only I would rise
stumbling and bang into every
day at the same time

FOR LUCY, TO EARTH

She who was
so tuned to light
now must lie so
stilled and mute,
who sped headlong
towards the day, the child
and instrument of sun
scarce mounted on the morning
air before
cast down to early
night and silencing of song, now lies
headlong in such dark.

She will need less
space than most,
Earth, in your partitioned place.
We can almost guarantee
she will prove
a gentle guest; mannerly
she always was, though young
in human company. She will not disturb
what's here. Earth, be gentle:
she will stay
lightly in this
stranger home.

Reminiscent of Jonson [illegible] . . .

HOMAGE TO ROBERT LOWELL

i

I have come home, like you,
to these high hills and this low
river, salt-bound and fettered:
I sense people shuttered
in these clapboard houses
standing at bay's
edge, that mere
gap in the ocean,
figure-
heads behind curtains starched like foam,
scrimshaw folks.

How beautiful the fall is here!
Tough grass and tigered lilies,
tumbled stone
walls, holey
and merciful to small creatures
looking to winter's
crannies (one winter here
is worth a dozen out-of-state) out of the wind.
Gulls turn on autumn's
wheel, we are all
gulls no matter what season,
but some are more nobly gulled than others.

ii

Who is to tell
who is to say
Old Puritan
what's to be done
to wit to who
(along the track that hollyhocks by day
and owls

by night laugh me down)
who'll sing
who'll dance
we wish to what
wisht the word
to sin
who's dune
who's dunce
let's bend
our hinges, crook our pins,
queer the changes
rest a while
us gulls
see and believe
scoff but deliver,
and good luck,
well done, and after pricks,
sleep time.

iii

Sin sin sin salt sin sin

iv

Man with the long twig on his tree
is buttoned up from less to more
and only breathes his branches when
his used
wife sleeps
at last and he can lie
at length trembling in his own
dream of his final whore.
But we were all of us green once.
Once we all whirled our pines
on that sublime, monotonous shore
and could be kind,
magnanimous even, to those smaller
patient pools that had, maybe, one crab
pink as a baby's toe, and one dead

starfish that some tourist
always took
home and let finish rot
on city-sooted window sill:
he did not know that gingko tree
was not what we planned, and wondered
why his salt trophy had the wrong
sweet smell, the marshy smell of blood
and not of semen:
our brains, at the tops of us,
breathe comments on the moon, and tidings,
brood on the sea-paths to earth
and without sensible light
can foam green leaves.

v

How can I say you are bound
to be Prometheus, or even
unbound, when you are the rock?
Your wound festers, though.
Rub salt, drink vinegar.
Suffer. Suffer.
Your open
vein leaks acid
and slight bloody show.
High up beaks circle on great wings.
Your iron eyes
draw them. Chained, you will grow
viridian like inland statues.
Your relatives in tennis shoes
will come to hang
a wreath on your private barnacles.
In winter your moss beard
will howl green into the north
by northeast wind.

vi

Your new widow walks
the icy path you built

on the top of your square house.
Only the iron rail
keeps her from tumbling over.
They say you've sent
her mad with rhyme. Walks,
walks, and does not look
down at all
out on that sea that never gave, but took.
She has grown more thin, she has grown more tall,
she is not the woman you knew,
you did not know her then,
she cannot know you now,
that she did she will not allow.
She is all of a piece, she is thin as glass,
she is tall as frost,
self-willed as a ghost.

While you sat brown in your study,
relying on metaphors
(pen, ink, paper, and the motion
of an arm across
an artificial horizon), did she
plan her roof-rise?
Some people use a weather cock.
You had your muse.
(When you first saw her, by the gate
into the summer field, she turned on you
and your green, your burning
her bruised blue gaze
like holes in ice
on a bright cold day.
So marred, you married her by God,
begot, and the steeple shook
the main part of the sky.)
Meantime motion-
less on the lawn down there
that paradigm of upward-running dark
New England nun
the solitary elm,
elegant, watchful, and withdrawn,
sank aged roots deep in the bitter snow,
and you indoors were tortured by your trust
and summer

visions of the swan your father took you on,
no common swan but godling's toy and carrying
garden varieties of Ledas leaning to leaving sailors
ignorant of Zeus and certain family
connections, and you, always the youngest,
always the anguished and the vulnerable,
charming and serious in your Seabee suit.

vii

Didn't you like
come on now
didn't you just enjoy
that mad being prisoned
for the term
with the grating like rhyme
like solid metre
so you knew where you were
where you were you were new
and you wanted to sing
in your little Bedlam
with the wool in your eyes
in your little yard wide,
so you sang and you graphed
and the walls ran true?
Didn't you?
Oh you conscious objector! You
sprung
you were sprung
you ran free
you sprang free
you staggered

, you,
our skunk hour, you our
black and white, striped with tar
and the white wash of your
innocence ignorance, towards the marble
marmoreal and through the arch,
old,
on the march,
the old poet-animal

we admire, we applaud,
but we cannot emulate
the wave of your inkstained paw
as you pass with your age
marked in pitch on your brow,
on your marble head,
your padded feet, such
a domestic, tamed creature for cause
(yet with your weapon,
your intact, virtuous reason).
Maybe you are the good badger,
and maybe
we have got our myths mixed.

viii

Yet I never.
You shed muses and disguises like worn wings.
What do you see without your spectacles?
You travel, scouting compass clipped
to a sad black sock. No wonder
rain slicks Paris, you bring your weather
with you. Cluny, Louvre, Notre Dame,
sides of the same
hotel door revolving.
Outside, you tip your head
and let a gargoyle douse your curls.
Berlin suits you better: dirty mist
under the lindens haloes Loreleis
in Dietrich kraut-coats. Papa, you were here,
or was it Tom? Prose can be sometimes helpful.
You can drown
your lineal sorrows in that eau-de-vie,
but wait for the real thing
the filthy-aproned servant with the leer
brings in, short-legged, with the beer
brown as the Kavanaugh at home.
That's where your needle quivers
to. Confess, in Rome,
that Michelangelo can go
from Newton to Dorchester on the cars
and still stretch that finger

out from Adam up to God.
A thousand candles melt towards that
small box wherein the smell
consists of Gorton's Codfish Cakes,
Portugee wine, and Him Who died
for Christ's (New England)
sake. Amen! Go, sin
no more.

ix

The dripping wax too much for you?
Poor Icarus. You were not meant
to be a saint in deed.
Empty, irresolute, ashamed,
you wander your own beaches
strewn with the grammar of your heart.
Your little hound
follows your heels, his tail a quill
between arthritic legs:
brush-cut, he quivers with his stubborn faith.
You turn away from January questions,
only a fool ventures such hoar North,
but your dog comes on. You miss a priest, but he
knows the odor of your overcoat.

x

I stand at the end of the pier.
It is winter for all of us,
you know,
we must beat our hands
together if we want to know
our veins are yet alive. Have you gone in
at last, are you working in the cottage on
translations of the dead by the dying sun, tilting
the imperial crown at chariots you make
appear on waves off Somerset?
They are not real to me.
I look down, you see,

I stand at the end of the pier and look down
and I see moving slime and old men
with furled umbrellas wrapped in kelp,
declining seaweed nouns, heaving
like flails, coiling like life
but ordered to wear galoshes,
and behind the Childs' streaming window
mermaids clash the dishes like cymbals.
I should not care myself for a place
where parrots spout like whales.

If you look back,
if you look back
to the still shore,
on the still shore
the quiet rock
leads light into itself.

TIMEPIECE

I had to take my watch
to be repaired
I took it down-
town to a Mister Stahl
(I got his name
out of the book)
his shop is let
into a wall
he wears a vest and yellow teeth
and his thoughts are all
underneath his green shade
just the same
I am terribly anxious about
my timepiece
Mister Stahl keeps on keeping it

It is a very fine
watch a unique
antique lady's
I inherited
Swiss gold handmade
he said at once
I wound it too tight
when I felt the mainspring go
I felt as though
I'd killed something
I think he knew
he put his eye
in looked it over
that I set with quirky fingers
inside his cage
glum shook his head
he doubted
I turned away not really
surprised
resigned
but then he called
me back permitted

his eye to drop
into his hand he said
he'd try although he'd have to
send away

that was OK
by me Sir I went out of there
I ticked on my own
Now
now I've run down

you see I can't believe
he means to give it back
I've called I've phoned
he puts me off the mainspring first
when that was fixed for after
that it was something else
and again something
else his smile
hangs in my air
the yellow smile of Mister Stahl
in his hole in the wall

and if ever he does
give me back my time-
piece I might not recognize it maybe
he's pawned it sold it off
in parts maybe
he's given it to
his granddaughter on her birthday

and I'll be left
I'm left
with a length of real
gold chain
and a golden hook
and nothing
to fasten to

except the yellow wall
that is the smile of Mister Stahl

ON THE POSSIBLE KILLING OF A THREE-MONTHS-OLD CHILD BY A RABBIT

i

News of the animal world
(listen, and breathe, Sheep Child)
from varying points of the US compass,
viz., from GREENPOINT, PENNSYLVANIA,

HUNTER IMPALES SELF, THEN
DIES (AP)–

A young man hunting deer
with a bow and arrow died Tuesday when
he fell from a tree, impaled
himself on one
of his arrows and bled
to death after walking
and driving for two miles, state
police said.
Police said
Robert L. Sholly, 25, Lebanon,
Pa., was on a platform
he had built in a tree when he dropped
his quiver of arrows. While climbing
down, he fell
on the quiver and an arrow
went into his thigh.

Viz., from FORT SMITH, ARKANSAS, BLAZING
RACCOON SETS CHURCH FIRE (AP)–

A raccoon, his fur
coat ablaze, strung a ring
of fire in grass around
the nearby Enterprise
Baptist Church, burning
the small building to the
ground.
Deputy
Sheriff Carl C. Coneley
said the raccoon
leaped out

of a trash barrel Friday
with his coat
on fire a few minutes
after a cleaning
woman dumped burning
debris into the container

ii

Was it raining? Did the street lights bleed
rosy haloes through the city mist?
The weather might be important.
Was it a beautiful mild
autumn night, with a few milky stars?
OH THE RED EYES OH THE VIBRISSA
hanging over the raddled couch.
and the fur, like cotton
candy, like the ghost
of the biggest snowman!

Where did it grow, how did it get itself
out of the cage, out of the
crumpled litter?
WAS IT SOMEBODY'S PET,
who was the friend?

Did the flesh
taste wafer sweet, like new
bread, like white
rose petals? From the little
stump, a rubbery string
drools, like the chewed
shred of a red balloon.
Sleep, baby.

NEW YORK (AP)–

Detectives said
George Owens Jr. and his parents were visit-
ing a friend in Queens yesterday and the
father and the infant went to sleep about
midnight on the couch. When the father woke
up this morning, his son was lying dead be-
side him. His right forearm had been chewed

> or ripped off, police said, and there were
> bite marks on his face and left leg. A rabbit
> was removed from the apartment and police
> were investigating the possibility that it
> had killed the child.

How's that, you masters, calm beasts
of the field? We are all closer
than you know, you thought you knew.
Children of the Lamb, unite, and pray
kneeling on your altar, earth,
for arrows, fire, and for ignorance.

CIMMERIAN

Cimmerian: one of a mythical people described by Homer as dwelling in a remote realm of mist and gloom.

i

The slow disintegration of the mind
is worse than sudden madness for the seeing,
that wraps the dreamer at a single stroke
away, away! and has the drowning done
too rapidly for fullest knowing.

To watch the water
fouled of that pure intercourse
of thought with image breaking into word
that leaps with wit the colored thread
tying the curving form to being,
and the mind

pulled slowly taut, too taut, too slow
and dredging out
dripping and heavy some poor muddish thing
to flop it panting on the bank
and slyly smile it towards
the still-sought approval, –

hello
hello
hello
say the nearly dead eyes,
the dying cornucopia mouth.
I cannot answer them,
I am weaving a wreath of hooks.

ii

Born untimely into May
this poor lady suffered cold

and she will go out, it seems,
in the same time
in the same way,
for she is dying of it slowly,
slowly,
with a pressure on her brain,
a glacier spreading over
matter of her mind. Was she then made
for snow, or rain?
                                        She wept,
I remember that
she did weep, her secret told
for those who cared to look
next morning in the heavy fold
of eyelid, swollen pulse at throat
like birdsong turned
sullen to ice. Is it of that stoppage
she is dying, also?
What did she want, beyond the lack of ill?
Need, to be brought to this
white immaculate
tight-sheeted private bed in this private room
where even the TV screen stays blank?
Maybe she's comfortable: outside translucent
veins siphon off
soiled yellow fluids from her body's vessel,
keeping her organs clear as God's eyes
washed by the death of slaughtered innocents.
She wanted sleep. Remember,
I remember that. She longed for sleep
like love.
                    That first day
I returned, she rose up
at my entrance
quite off her bed
and gave tongue to terror
Aagh aagh aagh
That was genuine If you want to see
your mother alive the other said
over the wire you had better come
at once I saw
what was meant She fell back, and my self
went round some corner.

I sit beside the bed,
child to the mother, older child,
and watch her sleep
that is like sleep and yet not sleep,
deeper than sleep yet not
yet deepest sleep while breath
snores along plastic pipes
with a yellow rattle, and the shutter of skin
flickers over the eye-
ball empty of dream and of reflection
dull, a mirror badly silvered
A sleeping beauty, lying, lines I knew
on brow, at lips, gone,
cheeks plumped with false
health, rosy even, prompting
numb wonder, simplest regret.
He, at the other side,
stretches out thumb like thorn to touch (horror) her nose!
"Get out of here," he growls,
and shakes his lion's mock mane,
"and I'll buy you a new hat,"
he murmurs. Booby! Tenderness
almost breaks him down.
He turns towards me. He begs,
"Take her hand. She likes
it when you hold her hand."
My cold hand
creeps across the coverlet
to hers, I take
her warm lifeless blanched
hand, wrinkled and soft as though by soap
and long water immersion, in my own.
Such courage! I'd soonest
stroke a live
leaf that a snake kisses in passing.
I hold on
"You think she knows?"
The snore. "She knows,"
he repeats, stubborn in love,
in self-reproach, in agony. In tears.
"She recognized you."
Yes. She did.
He leans to her. "Sweetheart."

A tone
of voice I never heard before but coming
from some love-letter past.
So, they were young once.
What else could be new?
They strolled beneath green showers of leaves,
he in blazer, she in white lawn, and I
cast the merest shadow in between.
Atone, atone.

iii

Whereas in fever fire
strikes me with its streams,
thought like a bright rippling
chain of snakes uncoils,
dazzles,
unbraiding hissing in my heightened
brain, blinds and cracks
over me its whips of deadly
play, ashes and metal
spitting from its tongues

so that I hoop myself
and stammer under beauty twinned
with terror in a killing rain,

now stand I fixed
by faulted love and colder
grief, helpless to charm
or tame, but drawn
under the goad of guilt that is
disordered
pride to finally fondle
grief
like asps to scape the gaze
of little lidless eyes
unblinking in the passing
shade of love: pride's darling
is brought down in fiery poisoned light.

iv

Once when I was a child in fever
near a winter sunset, she climbed the narrow stair
to gleam, quick and modest, in my room
with my supper tray, the evening
newspaper tucked beneath her arm
(the freckled arm summer and winter round
and strong of a country girl despite
her weekly marcel and her genteel air;
the arm that Mondays meant to hang out clothes
beautifully pegged to stretch the city
backyard to a snapping breeze, and did,
so that on Tuesday nights fresh sheets towards sleep
smelled of the silver iron as of dreams
and the sanest, cleanest sun, –
her washes were her miracles, she felt that pull
of art, and in her extreme
illness, while she was still at home
at home, my father, returning at six
one January day (he clung
to the normal routine; God knows
what she did when he was away) found her
wrestling in freezing dark
with an icy sheet like a white Styx or angel,
she winning, wearing
her dead farmer brother's overcoat, and grinning, –
of course there was more to it than that).
She came into my room
mine was a little room
it faced the West
it was a little room
but it was the best
they told me I hated it
mine was the smallest room,
not a tower.

"See the bright sunset,"
she said, and I understood a truce,
a pause in our lives' occupations,
and I looked
out of my fever's tired heat and saw the red
flaring strands spread live across the sky

out my window like high stretched membrane.
"Yes," I said. Whose was it,
drying out there in the cold?
Less did I see it, less that it was bright
than bloody, wind-inflamed, more than bright,
and which sank, sun like Jehovah's streaming eye
or earth its daytime moon?

I said Yes
often in those days.
She moved my burnt-out books,
Three Musketeers, The Snow Queen, Nancy Drew,
settled the tray, gave me the news.
"The old King is dead."

George V that would be,
in the shade of Mary.
Her eyes even then washed pale
blue stones, she still
because I was ill
(no one kinder then I have told, more gentle)
made cheerful speech, so that I thought
it must be indeed a fine thing
to be a king, and die
in the red winter sunset. *Pax*,
she put her nerve-thinned hand
on my forehead that felt skinned
by fever, and enmity
in the hollow died, love, long live the dead
long live
love live the dead
roses are red but white
too her veins ran cold
as that king died by fire
her ice communicates
I will be fierce and she
will die true.

v

It is light late now. Doves in evening
moan in rooftrees, smoothing

the last rough edges from the day.
Housewives have gathered white lilac from hedges,
swept doorsills, wished they could sweep the grass,
set children out like plants and brought them in
again against the treacherous early chill.
We have risen above all that.
We cannot get up and go down there.
We must wait up here within walls for somebody.
The little bell tings
a stone flung into a river of stale air
brings tidings to our sheltered, sour air
of lives smartly cracked or pried tenderly
from shells of soft creatures we shall never touch.
The little bell stings with its reminders.
Somewhere in firehouses men sit suspendered,
doors open, hunched over unyielding checkerboards.
An old woman in a clean dress has watered her
African violet,
and a child cries out unheard from a dream of lions.
When can we descend to their level?
Pulled tight like ineffectual angels
on our plastic lines we are held up
across from one another to each other
over the breathing body of our lives.
Through tightened lips we cry her mercy,
our turbanned lady where she lies,
her violated head shaved, cut, sewn
with tidy stitches over the havoc growth
that is so rich and rank it is not worth
the while of snipping saviors. Their fingers kink
at involuntary failure. She might smile,
now that she's shown her strength.
He tells me that in her last
months at home that is what she did:
she sat in the kitchen rocker and smiled
and chuckled at his effects
at the stove he had set her at
in the front of his mind for years:
she had laughed at his apron strings.
Also, she wrote a letter to her sister in Vancouver,
saying that he was dead.
How her long dimples must have bit into her cheeks!

Then her control went, and she defecated
an afternoon on the bedroom floor
before she slid under and the ambulance was called.
My father told me with some wonder
that when the firemen appeared in her room
with the stretcher, she, on the bed
by that time, smiled.
"Gave them a big smile!" he said. "As though
she was going to a party!" The Fireman's Ball.
What did she want, beyond what any of us
want: money, beauty, power? Why that odd hauteur
when the circumstances of my father's world
waltzed her in reach of them? Their perfume sent
her nostrils cold, she drew
gentility about her like a false
housekeeper's shawl and bowed her head over
ostentatiously simple
invisible embroidery. How she could ply that needle!
They murmured she was hard to know.
Once in a healthy winter when it snowed
she rummaged a square of black
velvet from another of her ages, summoned
me to the open casement window where we leaned
to spread the black patch to catch flakes,
each, she said, perfect, and no two alike,
perfection in the plan and in the execution,
she said, becoming excited with morality
while I saw only changes in the air to earth
the frozen pitch, star-shot
without sound, feather-soft down
from the breast of the owl gray sky
(four o'clock in the afternoon),
plume bristles from the flight of the Arctic fox,
shards of the great icefloe, and ashes
of the fire of sped virtues' light –
I stuck my private tongue out to receive
a flake quick and cool as a wafer
to my topmost earthen root,
but her hair blew in my mouth with the wind,
we were close, her strong
arm rosy with the challenge held
the lovely litter of silence on a shred of night.
How far from earth is air?

vi

That last afternoon, they said, the nurses said,
she would be studying her hand, raising it, so,
against Venetian-blinded light, a not unnatural,
they added, act of those in her condition.
The condition was mortal, of course.
It was not for better or worse,
it was wound with no moral choice, but was mortal chance.
That we were not there was chance, we were in fact
buying an aromatic box
of cigars at the Turks Head Club after late lunch
(we had to feed ourselves with heavy silver).
"I shall never forgive myself." His words.
So she studied: undisturbed
in her special torpor, in a stupor of learning
raised her hand, noted perhaps in her lobotomized
lopsided brain the queer fleshed brace
that let her fingers stretch apart the face
of treacherous air, who smiled and curled
itself instantly unseen
to membrane delicate as moth's
wings between the bones
like thicker twigs but more articulate,
as though trees had her veins.
Her bones could have done anything,
crawl sands, swim, fly, – they will take her far
from where she is, from what they are,
extensions of forgiven time in her they will carry
her out of herself and home
free to her element.
She will go back, but not the way she came.
Did she learn perfection is not bred
by blood but from the bone? Children,
we skip over our dead perpetually
with marrow knowledge of their natural state.
Whose labyrinth is lit
with torches for the speech of worms?
And afterwards the wedding feast.
She must be bride
in name only, escaping through the aperture
of dream she will run hard
through the wood (rivers of waters run

upward, wearing the trunks of trees)
to emerge at the edge of the field and leap
the gate mane flying, constellations
clamoring at her hooves, frightening the birds
who scatter like seeds from her fiery flower
that rides higher, highest, then gulping air
like ashes
spins down, rides, glides down
to phoenix rest in a nest of golden sheaves.

All right. But it may not happen like that.
More likely she will suffer,
she
suffered her hand to fall or allowed
it docilely to be put down, yet like
a child towards dark
and we not there
looked towards the door
and waited to be assured
and we not there
to be reassured
before her veins were bubbled out
and the globe of her eye
masked, asked
answer that all is safe, and she is good.

vii

One morning, tourists in the Jeu de Paume,
we checked our umbrellas and swarmed
in damp stockinged feet up slippery stairs
to view the wise old men.
We sliced through Van Gogh and saw
Manet through his model picnic. In a corner, though,
we came on other weather. "Death
of Camille," we peered through steam to read,
stepped back, and there she was,
seen slowly through her veil of snow.
Oh, she came,
ill, beyond old, but ill
the mouth gaped rouged for violets,

the eyelids pressed to themselves browned petals,
the chest crushed antique bouquets.
Sparrows through the eternal whirl of flakes
cried their plucky, desperate *Vite! Vite!*
Dying? She died long ago.
It is the idea of her
that is kept alive through the snow,
as though the young man of the glacier
impeccable in full evening dress
had her fresh with his boutonniere
and they two embraced
in the river of ice
in the mirror of sky
in their glass house roofed with the crystal boughs
of air their victim, jailer, discrete friend.
These lovers—I knew them well—are real.
Do not discount,
either, the plausibility of truth. Mountains move.

viii

It is your absence lies upon these landlocked hills,
the presence of the shadow of a cloud
which like a lowered hand to shadow thought
moves with the train, rests and then passes
with the thought like breath, to catch across a name
at the next unstopped-for station.
A piece of your signpost lodges at my heart, —
to my shame I am ashamed to say that word,
it is suspect, I must have it out,
yet it sticks in my throat: I am ashamed.
I am going home, I suppose, to the West
to leave you I have left before, vacating summer,
asking myself what new thing you have sent
ahead to make the lost salt tears rise to my eyes.
It is your absence softens me this time
and lets the hills swim while the rivers swell.
Look, I am going, we are going fast,
we have gathered ourselves, we are leaving behind
what is left of you in our merciless
progress deeper towards the sun. The plain

wears out the hills, the sky grows potent
hourly, we are ripping along the seams
of that quilt
pattern looks so real
you can almost reach out and touch
it, and the pelt
of grass that hides a rage
of insects like small birds (back home
that jay that laughed
blue from a branch of juniper), –
but everything else
is open here, no secrets, barns coffin
new grain (when they lowered you
the jay came out and laughed to the clods
of earth that struck you honestly),
houses boast new roofs.
Farmers walk crops like generals
who stride down ranks of nodding marble
gallused thumbs money dowsers.
Are you the hawk that rides above the yield?
That shadow passes, too. We go,
we have got away, we are moving on,
we have flicked our land-whipping tail past towns
called Nauvoo, Fickle, Antiville,
Kismet, Morocco, Hindustan
the stations no train stops at
no train ever stops at Flytown any more.
We are lengthening out, we are stretching our iron paws
towards the far phalanx, the rocky shields
that bank the sinking fires of the sun.
Almost within our pale single eye we can discern
at the very end of the world
certain small stick-like figures stooping and rising,
stooping and rising, burying day
and raising night in accordance with their task
whose appointer remains nameless by request
but whose beard overflows the peaks at dusk.
One of his eyes, brighter, is larger than the other,
an eagle is a speck of sand in its pupil,
his mouth whistles the whirlwind,
stars jump like fleas in his hair.
It is he whom we must pacify,

it is he who sucks our air
up from our butterfly lungs, thickens our throats
with his fear, sends our limbs sprawling in love
with his darkness, his beating of wings. His beak
caresses the murder of our journey to his light.
You are waiting here.

ix

How shall I blaze noon
being cold and dark as pre-dawn
down to my clay finger-
tips and nails of grayish horn?
No
cock shall crow me up nor the inflamed
and righteous burning
day's eye draw
or mark such mourning for its own.
I want no witness to my will to mine
the black ironic vein wherein I dwell:
I have a purpose now
to raise the grass above that mound
I trespassed in my going.
Yet I know what and where
your house is, what and who
creeps up your stair the while you toss
in your marshy bed amid your sedgey dreams,
and who slinks out before first light, to swing
itself from your backyard tree. I come
by night, by my own night, in stealth, yet bear
my particular phosphorescence.
I am your element, and I ravage,
I scavenge the graves of your worlds.

BEYOND THE SUMMERHOUSE

i

Journeys

A scorched leaf
stuck to its window (dirty)
of the slow
moving late departured train

my own head on its own
brain stem turns
stays reading that taut image
struck

on the streaked glass from the one
familiar tree
genus loathing species
loving—I know

those veins that tattered
reflective icon!
After three days
unspeakable conditions

the conductor calls my station
I take my suitcase down
disdain
his black wings his tarnished

medallion show
my documents correctly stamped
To Whom It May Concern
my ticket is continued

i

Arrivals

No one else
debouches here
this dust-ridden
wind-bitten signboard flapping platform

greets
the empty ticket booth
flutters the clock
stopped at twenty past

the benches bare the floor
even of spit
a school without pupils
who travels this way now

a ghost place
I go out again
to wait and see
that they have sent the trap for me

the pied horse spavined
heavy hoofed not ever
animal I was acquainted with
that patient bony head

nor driver either
hunched yet tall
his glance is sly his nails are long
his coat is borrowed like his grin

No Name is thumbtacked to his back
I do not ask but clamber in
he does not speak but slaps the rein
the horse takes slack and we begin

ii

Journeys

Landscape the flat of a knife
heat rising from
brooding upon that flatness
those reaped fields

that crows drop to
like charred gulls
to feed on culls of grain
under the gape of sky

our road runs straight
no lizard striped rock
no cracked tongued tree
to sing our progress on this plain

only the yellow constant
billow in our wake
hardly horizon save that in the mind
bruised lassitudinous

remembered band beyond
between blue and blue a sail
. . . salt in the eager wound
out of that whirlwind recall

the figure there amid the yield
walking a shade against the glare
pacing the distance alongside of us
where she has walked before

and since in jeopardy of sun
do not walk in the sun
barefoot through stubble
skirt kited up head uncovered

throat open
to the August assault
she must hear our chariot like a hive
our wheels

a thousand thousand bees
humming voices prisoned possibles
to spin her deaf
and rattles by

forget her forgot
she'll be walking centuries in her place
let the birds cry gold
showers of it baubles kisses

high-born lovers dissolving
like the brass green ring

their rainbow wings beat thin
dust in her blazing face

ii

Arrivals

Gates are set wide for us
(I am expected)
the drive narrower than I recall
weeds whisper our swift axle

hedgerows reach out to guide us
into the curve of the circle
the courtyard at last and the clatter
onto the paving stones

grass
spouts from the cracks
the fountain a fist raised dry
before the great cliff of house

—but stop!
He is taking me wrong
the wrong way around
away from the facade

the facade is what I want
orders have been confused
he'll not get my penny
I shall not disembark

amid scratching hens
and the contents of buckets
I know my rights in this matter
I shall enter

through the main portal or not at all
I am practically
a daughter of the estate
I tell you I am expected!

iii

Arrivals

In the pergola
laughter of restitution
a mistake a joke on us
among us nothing has changed

or perhaps change has occurred
but cannot be serious
no one has planned it
nothing is meant by it

a glass of warm tea
the plump girl proffers
her apron smelling of starch
and the clean freshly ironed sea

not far off–
does she have a ploughboy?
The pergola's in shade
a relief

these ordinary kind
faces attentive inquiring
the children's shouts outside
as they romp in the unmown grass

civilization! civilization!
"Our darling . . ."
"So much she's been through . . ."
Gently

he strokes his white silk beard
she amiably croons
both wear light linen
mourning sympathy

rails glitter in my eyes:
"My trunk has it arrived?"
Her pompadour shrugs slightly
jet black she retains

that vanity she spreads
her fine hands ringless
save for the wedding band
where is the ruby that I coveted?

"Dear—you have no idea
you may have to unpack yourself!
Are we finished here?
Just put the glasses on the tray

we'll carry in . . ." Such domestic flurry
he protests: "But the sunset
a most magnificent best of the season
they say—"

"The grass is damp already
call the children do . . . You
incurable then I must though we agreed
it was your responsibility—

Children children . . . time!"
I'll jolly him
tuck his arm under in the old fashion:
"Tell me

is there much honey this year?"
He shakes his white silk head:
"Too much rain in the spring . . . ."
His bones are brittle in their wrinkled sheath

iv

Arrivals

The huge whited shell
inside the same you would think
you could hear the sea in it
the snail growing and retreating

the grizzled wolfhound snarls
from the dry hearth or grins
our same three shadows swell
before us as we climb:

"You'll show me tomorrow?"
"We'll re-acquaint you with the place . . . ."
"That driver?" "Got hold of
a wrong scheme . . . ." I nod we agree

some whip in each of us
in his niche the blackamoor
hoists his dead torch
the lamp unlit hangs on its chain

her skirts a skein of sound
voice a silk winding: "But for tonight
for tonight she must rest . . . ." A chime
oh do not let me dream

i

Soundings

I meet her on the terrace facing West
she too is combed and dressed
for the duel
we sit at the glass-topped table

her wrist pouring out stops lies:
"You slept I trust you slept
well?" The cup and her concern
I can thank her for those

he is approaching below
by a vegetable walk
his skylight gaze catches us
jauntily

he waves his stick: "A moment!
Mark me as I progress
save me a crumb!"
She murmurs: "You would never guess . . . ."

"What?" "He takes it seriously . . . ."
"What?" "He will say it is
a fox in the chicken run
a rat in the granary

a poacher in the wood
a thief in the orchard–pah!
Mere crutches! Lies..."
"But why?" She shrugs: "Fear . . ."

"Of what?" "Judgement–
of poverty which is death–
maybe of paradise..."
"But this is paradise!"

I falter how she pursues:
"You say that for you see it
as it was you years ago
on holiday you are not

what you were we are not . . . ."
"The children they don't change–"
"You've noticed? you're quite right
they're in a different scheme . . . .

Oh I could show you more
things you ought to have seen
before now and now
you will have to find

yourself paradise and hell
the snake with its tail tongued to its mouth
rolling downhill–
I know enough of both!"

"And where does limbo come?"
A blind falls shut on that
no further word
from that quarter

"Here we are here we are!
Prepared are we for our stroll?
We're promised each to each?"
So droll today he seizes

her cup and drains it: "We're off . . . ."
"Wait–the children

where have they got to what
are they playing at?"

"Nests
of nettles I daresay haha!
Poor little beggars in the summerhouse . . .
My dear?"

iii

Journeys

So we set out on foot
how far from yesterday
we travel not true North
the needle's quivering tip

on the mental map but a limping
compass circumscribed
subject to
his game limb (a shooting accident)

diminishing returns
burned barns and pilfered bins
drought or flood
always at wrong junctures so the kine

drop their young stillborn
crops decay in the leaf
at midnight horses go lame
arbors wizen at noon

shamed articles to grief
I listen as I am meant
trail his hooded whimsical
track with its bitter

trivial sincere travail
nothing brave about it
a sort of crippled bravado seeking sidewise
approval of apologies

his voice sawing on like the caw
of a crow telling blackened beads

he would overwhelm my history with his failure
I allow it him freely

but at the chapel bell
at an hour of my choosing
he shall do penance
he shall kneel and I shall pray

ii

Soundings

Elsewhere in early afternoon
(my foiled priest has gone in
to rooms she continually
exits from)

I am spying
my roots like willow
my branches in disguise
the childish stream of prattle

enters my leaves: "Your name
what is your name today?"
"My name today is Ben . . . ."
Amused: "What does Ben do

today?"
"Fetches stick and growls!"
And to the other the same:
"What is your name today?"

"My name is Bet I am the doll—"
"Ben must take Bet
by the throat and shake her so—"
"To hurt her?" "Just a bit . . .

She must get down and beg
for mercy . . . . Oh
well done!" A slight clapping
as at chamber music

and then the snap of steel:
"What is my name forever?"

Syllables on the stream
sighing the ripples of:

"Lilla . . . Lilla . . ." I lean close
through my foliage Lilla it is
unchanged my favorite
in charge

charming in white
eyelet and hazel switch
the pupil stitched black through the iris:
"Lilla tell us

why we are not allowed
to wander why they snatch us back
from the wall and the gate
the hedgerows miss us and the shore–"

What can my favorite say?
She takes a breath begins her lie:
"A guest is here who does not know
she is the cause of our disease

we seem the same as when we were
she does not tally us as ghosts
nor realize she is one of us
she catches only glimpses of–"

"What shall we do to her?"
"What does she want of us?"
"She wants us live
my dears she wants us where

she taught us how the world was round
and empire red she wants
things simple she wants things polite . . . ."
"What shall her name be soon?"

All my leaves tremble at her smile:
"She'll dowse for it with the wand
she'll walk the estate over
with her dainty shoes!

After exploring of the cave
after the fire on the shore
(we'll wrap her in green leaves
a poultice to her scars)

when she has learned
or when she has been taught
we may give her a clue . . ."
"What can we do besides?"

"Pray the fine weather holds
play tricks in biding time
and promise to be true . . . .
She shall be satisfied!"

v

Arrivals

Tea-time and the doctor the one
official the other not
riding his sorrel at an easy trot
up the drive his soft

fedora dropped across his suede
vested interest
pince-nez informality that goatee
hhm hhm: "I find you as I imagined

assembled in the belvedere
the family plot
my joke you're looking uncommonly
. . . . since you insist–"

She calls out at once:
"Maizie! We want another setting . . . ."
Flashing with laughter:
"What would you suggest?"

"My treatment seems to be working!"
"Delightful you recall
our guest of long ago
she was no older than–

here's the girl now . . . ."
He bows cool as a knife
at our meeting how he is deft
how he squinted:

"Hot water quick!
These servants these days . . ."
She's right I could have done better
I shall remain demure

watching her fan-like hands
hover
white doves among the tumblers
I am of course wearing black in my position:

"I fear I am putting you out
shutting my surgery for the hour
wanting speech with coevals . . . ."
He pinches his nose: "Weary work

mine bumpkins
pitchforks grindstones scythes
kerosene childbirths by lamplight—
ah that's delicious!"

He wipes his neat moustache
sets his glass down with a thump
like a blunt instrument on a kitchen table:
"Where are my godchildren hiding?"

"Planning tomorrow's picnic I daresay
you'll come? You'll be wanted certainly!"
"Count on me . . . ." His fingers drum
he hums a tune his nails have grown

iii

Soundings

Next day however rains
the gardens fume
from my blurred window
trees droop with damp

the summerhouse assumes
a Chinese attitude
indoors the dog whines and yawns
he naps and she winds yarn

nothing to do but explore
search rooms try locks
what a large house this is!
How many portraits of the dead

passed over by the brush of time
so much yearning furniture
shrouded in dustsheets and regrets
a queer bourne this hush!

Soundless up the attic treads
crouch
ear to the panel thumb to the latch–
if I should catch them

at their mischief of
boxes and trunks in exile
Lilla parading in my shawl
the boy in my tartan the girl in my sash

my henna wig mismated–
by the keyhole my eye fits
only Lilla reading to
them clustered at her plaided knee

they listen like birds:
"'So then
they flew over oceans and islands
over lakes and woods and the cold

wind whistled where wolves howled . . . .'"
Angelic
we are all enchanted: "'The black crows
flew screaming . . . .'" Charred

gulls under the gape of sky
under transparencies of circumstance

I grope the stair beside the twisted rope
someone should light that lamp

i

Viewings

Amid anonymous monocles
perambulating
young ladies in waists and villas
we are preserved

perceived in wicker chairs
"At the Summer Residence"
in gazebo ease
"North of" after croquet

(a mallet tilts across his knees)
how genteel
the doctor clicked
she said and kissed me

we must take care he agreed
the wolfhound grinned—
I would have
buried it under three stones

but they persuaded
how we must think of the future
the children have not changed
where the light falls

the temple retains that fatal hollow
their eyes do not reflect
except the sky's pale gift
they are thieves too

twine their art
about you like the nightshade vine
the cold wind could whistle
they would assert its warmth

they could cut you to the bone
meaning no harm truly

you could sicken and die
courting disaster and applause

I am trying
to see myself clearly in the group
surely
I am there in the corner

of the camera's report
my black dress shows plainly
yet at the explosion
I must have flinched

or the photographer
bungled I have no features I appear
to be leaning forward
warning or seeking to warn

i

Fêtes

The day appointed and the laden breeze
draws up live voices at the dawn
scatters the ashes in the grate
the soft occasional

fumbling on shingle of the tide
filling the far rock pools
recovers resonance and wrack
and on the mantelpiece the row of shells

cowrie and mitre
moon snail and virgin nerites
echoes
remnants of naming of things—

Weltschmerz au revoir
baskets are being packed
cloaks and staffs called for
also parasols

everyone drinking coffee standing up
the children darting and quarrelling

everywhere everything in a word
normal on schedule here's the tumbrel

we scramble in with our baggage
Maizie has plucked a rose
for our driver blushing he starts
we are hurled backward what a flourish

what a spectacle! Hens scuttle
the dog howls
us down the lane and out the gates
as though he knows our fates

as though we are not already
having negotiated the turn singing
he beating time with his stick
she thrumming alto cicada

Lilla
bawls like a little drunk
in my ear the children shriek
impossible to keep the tune

the driver's shoulders heave
he's in disguise it's obvious
a mile away
we're whirling by

the figure walking
fold on fold the field
alongside the smoking road
she has moved up on us

stalking
extending her hold
sighting us vigil wise against the wind—
dust in her blazing face

ii

Fêtes

The end of the road to the sea
at the sea the end of the land

the low bluff promontory
the tip

leading into
earth into water and the airy waves
the skirmish to halt
halloo!

Hats off!
The doctor leaps down brandishing
shouting we slide to surround him
we knew it a success

he rang the bell with us
a merry scene
the ancient concertina
the horse's girth

wheezes accompaniment
to our unloading impedimenta
impatient the sea gavottes
the tide is high

the water blue dazzle
shall we be able to bathe
to perform our ablutions
for the once we plead

the duty of pleasure we can feel
already the plunge the splash
our skin tingles imagining
that impact while she poses

apart withdrawn
white under white umbrella
and the paternal or avuncular
frown

advises first things first
the driftwood if we want the fire
we want the fire
must be hauled

impaled
log tree root and spar
towards darkness the bonfire will show best
against darkness

they will be able to see it for miles
from their black ships or flickering
cottage windows
so he chuckles

settles his chin on his stick to supervise
this gathering in his hectare
and we fetch
lumber under the sun:

"Is it ready yet?"
"It is taller than we are!"
Oh he would have it to heaven
if it were left to him

but the doctor splendid in shirtsleeves
heaves the last log into place
his eyeglass ribbon ripples
he clashes his palms together

the hairs on his arms golden wires
she strolls through filtered light
over bone-white pebbles
she swishes towards him: "So?"

"Finished for what it is worth!
A monument to be consumed . . ."
"Monuments
should be consumed . . . ." Superb

she starts to turn away
he parodies a bow they do not touch:
"Shall we swim then now?"
"You may–I've done with such . . . ."

This time she does
fierce and indifferent turn

bereft
he shrugs and hollows his bright hands

about his red lips and bellows
released
flinging off we arrow to reward—bemused
the crow on the fencepost watches

iii

Fêtes

Half-clothed in this loud embrace
trammeled boisterous by the shock
of the element we tumble
we shout in the welter

they swim like eels
teasing winnowing the water
or like finny creatures nipping
at weeds and thighs

their slight wet teeth
they lure me out from the shallows
I flailing when I go under
his arms bring me up

gasping I am briny
my hair gushes over his wrists
the sun glows like kerosene
the clouds blister like steam

they surface
laughing they treadle
the buoyancy Lilla lays
a kelp frond on my breast

they help me staggering to shore
their bodies glisten with salt
lithe as though newly arisen
they prop me against the pyre:

"Mademoiselle—" "Good girl—"
As though it happens every day with him

("'Weary work mine'")
they race back to their element

their games
she approaches slowly with her basket
having furled her parasol
and struck it between two stones

from another direction
he also limping they converge
saying simply and offering
nourishment that we must

after such experience accept
I am asked to trust
a piece of bread a glass of wine
let the others sport

let them dally in the surf
we shall assent they imply
to the shale's hard comfort and confer
concerning our identical impotence

i

The Cave

Echo echo *ecce*
wrenched and infinitely injured
voices ricochet
from shelves and corners mock

and hoot mimick
birds at aurorean carol
animals at dusk
snufflings (if we have met walls

fingers come wet away) and human
susurrations
in the interstices
hum

silence
the silence

the silence runs
like water in the dark

over the rock of itself
within this rough dome of this dark
I stumble
something is thrust

at me instantly he lends
he is lending
bending towards me in the avocal silence
he lendeth me

his stick
which I strike
against a stalactite like a bell
hollow the knell redounds

from that inverted steeple
bleak and deep the toll
recoil
fooled foiled again I reel

from behind that perverted pillar
Lilla's laugh rings out
soft
peal upon peal–

I must stand out against
keep my wits remember
that I am practically
remember my justifying vow and my possession

now of the taproot therefore of the tree
that wraps the cave in its talons
up there
in that other cave

innameable immanent
I shall retain what he gave me
in the name of
in the name of

iv

Fêtes

We struggle out
half-blinded blinking and ragged
tattered at nerves' ends
under the jangling rays

In this din this radiance
against what must happen
what has happened already elsewhere
in the world–

I mean the dying of the day:
"We must prepare!"
Her hurly-burly
so she will clap us

will she
into good spirits will she
beguile us would she dare
project on this shore's scrim

enacted scenes
of innocence and joy innocent
because of joy earnest
because of innocence

she cannot gain our gaze
our gaze does not reflect
it is waiting for the fire
to fasten upon the fire

our ears cannot hear
being already attuned
to the attenuated crackling of the air
such words as she might have spoken

such music she might have made
dry like foam on her lips
within the sullen hour
halt

would I help if I could
(" 'So much she's been through' ")
the children fret and chafe
Lilla draws them with her

foresighted
she has brought a toy
she has hidden among the rocks
she shows them

I would have shown them
leaning forward warning
or seeking to warn
my black dress billowing a black sail

on this stony ground
with my stick I would have
I would have tried to trace with my stick
the first letter of their alphabet

The Fire i

A zone of dusk
the purple thickens the sea
the wind has subsided:
"Soon? Is it to be soon?"

"Very soon now . . . watch for the star
the one particular star
that wheels into position
there at the mid-horizon. . . ."

"Will the moon come too?"
"I if I were you
would not count on the moon. . . ."
Far out the sea shivers silver

as though someone has lit
a single lamp in the darkened cave of the air
a lantern in a ruined barn at night
a flare on a rustic table it blooms out

the pile looms behind us
anticipatory
we have crept
from our various shelters

to stand before to stare
at the soft refulgence
presently many stars
glitter less faintly

who will strike the match
our counterpart
limping and wincing he lofts
the small box

he carries the coffin of little lights
marries
the tinder to the flame
shifts it tenderly

ceremonious
into the heart of our driftwood
furnace that catches
instantly what colors

it is the salt rose ochre
the speech of blue tongues
leaping
from log to log consuming

a dance dance dance
savages stamp
high haigh haigh higher
oh we would have it to heaven

our arms beseech like branches
our feet beat upon the stones like metal
sparks fly from our ignited eyes
as the fire mounts we break

off to dance on our own
we whirl glowing we burn with the element

molten our veins our vitals tremulous
(only her leaf is white)–

the children's mouths open as they tread
buoyant and lambent in the noise
in the roiling welter
possessed

I throw my stick in like a crutch
to be blessed it is spun right up
a feathered spear a straw
in the roaring of timbers

he hops towards me
his arms outstretched
the heat lifts his hair like ash
our arms beseech each other like branches

ii

The Fire

Lilla dancing stumbles
the doll the wax object
hurtles from her grasp into
that inferno her face blazes

I rush I shall rescue
my favorite
I put my hand in
snatch what is hers

what doll what mask what pain
it is nothing but my own
I cower I cover my features
the dripping wax from my fingers

blisters
my face hardens grows older
instant by instant I have known it
but in no mirror of mine

I have pain to endure
the doctor works nimbly: "You will seem

yourself in no time. . . .
There will be no scars. . . . *Calme-toi!"*

So: I am being taken care of—
but what is my name
what is my name forever?
What nervous wind stirs in the embers?

i

Departures

By the red artifice of coals
the picnic is over
she collects her parasol
the children have their souvenirs

I am retiring in disgrace
her skirt says without a word
he disagrees I nod we agree
then we have made that peace

together we meet at land's end
the hooded ferryman
hired to oar us home
around the nightbound coast

below the cliff wings cut
suspect shapes
hover crying of oceans and islands
over our heads

at the cliff's top a private fire
like anxious tropic birds
in a strange climate flits
in a cage of shadows a figure

devotional
as our craft
slips so far beneath her
dividing the spineless waves

a brand in a long arc falls
hissing across our bow

the boatman veers—a momentary
phosphorescence—

his shoulders indicate
no more than that
(I cannot read
the placard on his back)

a burning bone dazzled out
the children huddle sleepily
clasping their treasures
she sits upright

as on a bench the boat is bearing
across the dark lawn he mumbles:
"No further word from that quarter. . . ."
She: "What did you expect?"

vi

Arrivals

At the dock he pays the boatman off
(I never saw his face
but his eyes gleamed like a slave's
behind the black bandage—

he bit each coin):
"Until next time!" Under night's blanketing
the lightly jarring sound
of retreating oars: "Next time!"

"Children children . . . Lilla
look after the little ones do
they stagger on the path
how they are weighted with stones!"

She is sullen scarcely more
than a child herself when I return
I shall make sure to send to her
a gift of some value to atone

for the loss of her plaything
a book would be most instructive

the book russet-bound with pages
the color of wasps' nests and waterstained

on the fly-leaf
written in spider's drift she will find
intertwined our names a nice conceit
she will be disappointed

vii

Arrivals

This country has no moon
but the birch trees we go between
glimmer weakly like photographs
of dressed women of another siècle

among them we pick diffidently
our way not talking
as in a museum of the future
we do not credit these trees

how smoothly she moves
propels us out of the woods
onto the sweet grass before the summerhouse
the doctor lounges puffing his cigar:

"I got back early by moonlight
the horse stepped right along. . . ."
The rose in his buttonhole
blooms black in the bud

Maizie emerges blushing
her apron smells fresh she smiles
takes his arm in the new way
she frowns and we go on

towards the house the huge
whited shell
lit up as for a festival
we press on towards the facade

iv

Fêtes

The fountain plays such tunes!
Village musicians
scrape and blow
crickets and staghorn beetles on the terrace

from the plump balcony the mayor
regales us in patois following the speech
such a spurt
the moss is annihilated

carp raise their heads in the basin
in the courtyard
they are singing in stanzas
heavy boots clump the rhythmic pavement

the dog wildly barks waltzing
I receive many compliments
a drunken peasant bestows the prize
a chaplet of milkweed pods

it is exhilarating
being at one with the crowd
beneath its uniform exterior
my marble face might have veins

the blood might beat in my encapsulated brow
like little gongs in a village church
quick quick quick quick
the candles chant in my kindled eyes

ii

Departures

Cockcrow
cockcrow
cockcrow
once twice thrice from the unseen dunghill

at the first crow of the cock
the violins shy like frightened horses

the drum clots suddenly
a crack appears in the main portico

at the second crow of the cock
"A storm?" she queries swaying past
in the exalted mayor's arms
at the third crow of the cock

the dancers scatter like rinds
before the whirlwind
carriages pelt headlong
down the avenue lanterns gibbering

passengers striving to fasten the curtains
at each other's throats
in the confusion
in the convulsion

the carp are extinguished
the fountain swallows itself
insensible
the mayor sprawls in a ditch

she has twitched her robe about her
fled indoors I pursue—
the blackamoor
hoists his dead torch

that lamp is almost out
his body dwindling from the twisted rope
could I arouse this household
she is there above me

bald as a darning egg
toothless and hunched
at her empty safe
unhinged—

"Thieves have got in. . . ."
Where is the ruby that I coveted?
"My treasures! My treasures!"
My heart's chamber pulses red

iii

Departures

Mist
rises like incense from the hedgerows
into the burning field of morning
the furrowed road

spills dust from my heels like pollen
my road runs straight
no figure paces mine
my shadow is my own

no sentinel
marks my progress
barefoot through stubble
daring to walk in the sun

skirt kited up head uncovered
throat bare to the august assault
such journeys always
end in leave-taking

iv

Departures

On the platform the doctor stammers
of luggage and traps
("The horse stepped right along")
I interrupt:

"You wish to wish me well?
I thank you for the charity. . . ."
I can afford these trifles now:
"And she?"

"Will be walking centuries in her place. . . ."
"No pity?" "None!" "The children?"
"None . . . No—none!"
Rails glitter in my eyes:

"No harm
no harm was meant I swear—" I swear

they could cut you to the bone
meaning no harm truly:

"How the wind blows out here
enough to dry your marrow!"
Grit between my teeth
I mount the iron steps

present him my countenance
pitiful he is so changed
I enter the narrow cage
and the iron door clangs to

iv

Journeys

To Whom It May Concern:
We are inching South
like the black finger of a glacier
under unspeakable conditions

food is thrust at us through windows
some have fought over water
there are rumors of pox
still one must persevere

I too have erred I confess it
between times I doze
nod off
dreaming of children and a summerhouse

this heat is stifling
heat lifts my hair into ash
I stretch my arms towards them beseeching
crying out into their dreams

"Civilization! Civilization!"
A scorched leaf
tattered
reflective icon

I thought you were real my darlings
you were only the shadows of my eyes

that opened once fitfully
widened in fear and suspicion

and closed again like flowers
blank as that sky before snow
meanwhile
my head on its brain stem turns

stays reading
my documents in order
farewell farewell
I shall write from Genoa

already I hear the sea wind
slapping the sails towards the new world
the gulls
circle high in the bright blue cave

Beginning with Dickinson's journey
with death & ending in a
[illegible] of the holocaust.

NEW ENGLAND

Stones
are the sheep of these
hillsides
and fog
is the wool of these stones

POEM OVERHEARD
IN A MAINE DOCTOR'S WAITING ROOM

"I never go out in weather like this
I never go out in weather like this
I was married on the shortest day
of the year fifty years ago and that's why
I've never forgotten it
my great-great grandmother married when she
was sixteen two families pioneered
pioneers in Limestone
I get so cold at night
my bones ache and I can't move so I come here
and the doctor gives me something
they had no shelter for the only cow in Limestone
that first night so the young bride flew out
from the covered wagon and pegged a quilt
a brand-new wedding gift around the cow
during the night it snowed
and in the morning when they went out
they saw the steam
coming from under the edges of the blanket
the bride was milkmaid and that very day
the young lads and the bridegroom
built the shelter"

SINGULAR NIGHT

My mouth tastes like a barn.
My conscience sleeps or does not
in the other room.
Down the way a dog howls.
I read a story of my life,
how dull, how instantly
understood. Wrong was done,
not to someone but to something,
some notion.
I dismiss Christmas, mistrust spring.
In a chagrined town the water
through the back window falls loudly
over the weakened dam.
Cars pass in front,
creasing the wet street.
Homesick, home,
his dream plows toward a station,
mine turns the headlight on.

STAYING OVER

That night in your apartment
I washed my face in Breck shampoo
your towel said 9 to 5
every day of your work week but the tiles
shone spotless on the bathroom floor
where the wallpaper had peeled by the light switch
an old water lily bloomed again
was it surprised
under the kitchen bulb you read the *Times*
I drank gin amid
your poems
later I thought
to water the hanging plant before we went to bed
in your tower window

THE COMMUNITY

Town like this Northern remote
used to many snows weather and spirit
hard to tell unless you've lived here long
who's what sick sane ill well
what are the marks of condition?
Some people you see more often or notice them
you notice each other
yet often give no sign

1. THE SHUFFLING MAN
it's our secret how he sets the trap
in each shoe huge for agenbite
oh he is ugly pendulous
lower lip like time denied and hanging there
his body
struggling through the air that I am free to shape
to me he bows his curragh back
struggling home from the shops
he lives alone they say he does beautiful
tatting I should not be surprised
if by lamplight
he copies Plato out in his own hand
while I search the cave
he knows a shadow when he sees one

2. THE LADY WALKING OUT a wraith
with hair unnatural but it is all
hers it seems
to grow on sight it coils it mounts itself
in spirals Brobdingnagian white snails
surely it battens on her brain
looping her ears her frail peninsula of neck
and makes her eyes bulge pale
blue out of her white
face as she walks beneath her hair bravely any
afternoon neat in dress and manner past
nodding flowers her body
a rail her legs and arms

pickets   a fencepost
what does the doctor say townspeople
turn up their palms   she is brave
can hardly be loved   cannot be feared
next season may sprout leaves   two birds
may fly out from my eyes   as we meet like trees
walking in opposite directions

3. THE MAN WITH THE WEN
ON THE STEPS OF THE REALTOR'S OWN firm
lounges   that bloody star between
his real gaze gauges   ruby magnet pulling in
town gen   ambulance fire engine hearse
suicide murder once in a while the Sunday roast
the bank president
today a child   grubs a piece of dirt-
candy from the curb   Quit
that   nasty   ugh   she hauls him off
we witnesses I look him straight
in that orb   he looks away
but recognizes   his ruby glows what other
sparrow dares to peck such fruit?

4. Comes with her headlong rush down the nave of elms
THE EGGSHELL GIRL ON HER BICYCLE too late
for any school   yes she is slow yet pedalling so fast
imagine if she fell off
her mouth would go O
her cranium crack
and a little yolk trickle onto the sidewalk
every day she rides it's therapy also collects
picture postcards she has forty-four
Katahdins at sunrise   Mother confined
to the wheelchair gets around
enough to dust the mission oak   turn the diurnal page
of the hymnal with a terrible methodistical
zeal   the daughter whizzes by her continual
anxious expression as though important events are taking place
just beyond her peripheries of perception
the arpeggio from St. Mary's tower
ripples out pigeons in blue habits
in the pursuit of angels

LOOT

What risks we take in transportation on this earth!
Given late March, a kiting sky, fiddlehead air,
we mount the morning bus to Old Town, Maine.
Winter-worn coats unbutton and our minds
simply because of the sun and our moving situation
quicken, vision also; the sight
of our driver's sandwich wrapped with his slice,
on the shelf above the steering-wheel, of the cake
still warm from his clean moist wife's oven
unparallelled in the Western world.

We stand, pay, are rung out, delivered
onto Main Street—Woolworth's shall see us,
Cutler's and Davis Drug behold us—look,
I'm skimming in Mukluks, slush to my ankles,
seeing such faces, some newly hatched, some still chinked,
peering under such hats, taxidermist specials.
Oh, I forgot the fish!
Yes, ma'am, up from Cushing early this A.M.
Huge flipper of his hand insouciant. His voice
gurgles like clam flats.

The nearby river runs high here this time of year,
greedy among polluted roots,
smelling of pulp; the waterfall
yellow as leather. Cold the chill stale.
Why are these shelters always set in shade?
One bundle too many, as usual.
A couple with a child has come to wait. We wait.
Her eyes burnt out; he lights up
a Camel, coughs. Pretty child,
maybe four years old, a pity,
but then think better, she may marry
instead of the mill its son, climb in cathedral white
out of the thinness, they are thin,
cheap-clothed like gaudy sparrows. Saturday nights
the pint of red-eye at the kitchen table
they sip by turns until they empty it; the child

on the cot near the stove covers her unmarked features
with an arm perfectly articulated,
sighs once in skim-dream sleep
where whistle never splits the pre-dawn dark.
He blows his nose in his fingers, by which we comprehend
the bus arrives, but we, she says,
with a smile that could lay wide another's brain,
shall walk in the park awhile before we go home.
That is what she says. Good luck, she says.
He coughs, grinds his butt out, clambers up.
We clamber up.
They will walk past the ruined bandstand on cinder paths.
Going home
a glimpse of the vine stripped and shackled to a railing
nailed to winter. On the bridge
the tall fence against the wind.

NIGHTWALK

"This lassitude,
this filthy languor,
this inability to laugh or weep or to decide
not to decide–
going on now for weeks of weather
inward, bland,
neither ennui nor anomie,
neither honest snow nor cheating rain
but cloudy, heavy, gray of gray,
the wearing on of day to unaccomplished day,
a kind of mononucleosis of the will.

"So last night, not unsleeping yet not yet asleep,
I got up out of what I had assumed
a bed humanly warmed, and crept in dark
downstairs, Lady Macbeth of Main Street,
the Bovary of the block.
The household
breathed deep and innocent around–
why should it not? These dreamers are real,
at least they dream real dreams. Outside,
it snows. The real glass paperweight
is gently shaken of the world.

"I know each step here, where the creaks are,
I know each passage through each room,
I have made this household, these rooms,
these children and their dreams, and him
and his, mine. Out of myself. Now I am hungry,
not for food, but for what might be mine
only. What greed,
in a place where children die of hunger.

"I open, delicate, diffident, novice to this greed,
the wide white door.
The little bulb blooms like an icicle.
Such stuff
we fill ourselves with! Plastic cheese, pizzas,

store bread, lettuce like counterfeit
money, hard fruit, something called
Grandma's Warm-Up Blueberry Turnovers—
and, of course, milk. From cows, we may presume.
Milk first, then. What we've had drummed earliest
into our infant bellies. It tastes smooth, and cold,
we have grown used to the coldness of milk, we
have made it a virtue, the smoothness of cold
whiteness in the childish cup. So,
emptied of thought, so
easily satisfied, I lick off my mustache.

"The door gapes all this time, the bill will rise
with this midnight feasting . . .
In clear as false air wrapping, like a new
fashion for some emperor's friends in vogue
a pound of hamburger
packed like solid measles. I pick it up, disinter
it, weigh it in my hand as an intern might
a brain disengaged. But cannot wait
and ravenous break the transparent membrane with my teeth,
spit the wrapping out, take the chunk of raw
meat into my jaws, and chew. Salt,
salt, it needs salt, and my eyes
are doing that at last, the liquid runs
down onto the meat. It's true, it's true,
the flavor is improved by tears.

"In the crooked rocker the cat sleeps
and never stirs to welcome me to his professional
community. His black-and-white
plush covers an earlier nocturne.
My mouse, my weasel I had to buy
to savage it again. Even its red
color is injected, I understand, but I understand
it is what I make do with.
The rawness and the salt are perhaps
a beginning.
And my zestful teeth are sharp.

"Strength, strength,
and newness in the blood.
Close the door softly on the light

and sneak,
a walking owl, up to my nest.
My eyes grow big in dark. The snow
still falling keeps my kingdom fresh.
My beak
parts in a killing smile, and salt like sweet
sand rests on my rasping tongue. In the morning
they will say how well I must have slept."

LIVES OF THE POET

i

The poet lets the cat
out
by the ordinary
door

ii

The owl is the only bird who
reminds me of a cat
it is the eye
like a single agate
cut in two
by a frugal crafter

iii

It was not the fault of the gnat
that he flew
onto my eyeball
as I
was gazing at the Parthenon

iv

Down at the cove
of the seven sycamores
even the fish are singing
because the girl
in the red dress
is coming

v

My friend said Mirrors
don't wear out you can
look into one for years

and it shows no change
think of that
she said I did

vi

So much rain this summer
even the fleas
have become dispirited

vii

Toad
like a hackberry leaf
under the mulberry tree

viii

Half of the berry tree is dead
the other half has never borne
so heavily
I could almost believe
it speaks to me

ix

Hear the crows'
black
barking in the wood

x

Suddenly the Chinese elm
sheds its dark
crown of birds

xi

The heel of my shoe
squeaks like a cricket
across the stone floors
of the autumn

xii

On the side lawn
sweating in the spring
the poet kneeling
grubs the teeth of lions /i.e., digs dandelions

THIS PERSON

This person that I knew changed her dress
every afternoon at four o'clock,
having washed her private parts
in the black-and-white
tiled genteel bathroom
and put perfume on of a pale floral scent,
to sit on the back porch swing under the green-
and-white awning to wait,
clean hands in fresh lap,
for only she knew what.
For years and years she did that,

and it was only my father who drove in
in the Studebaker, later the Buick, never
a Cadillac, which would have been
ostentatious, but his father
would have loved it, not being suburban,
simply a big frog
in a village puddle: him with his cupola
and his columns and his bonhomie,
his binoculars to watch the big boats
in the channel—I sometimes thought
it was him she waited for, in a queer fashion
during visits, they got on.

He might have understood, supported
what the other, darker and more nervous,
had cut off at the root. Inverse snobbery.
We are better, so we live worse. And she,
remembering cutwork and chromos and raspberries
floating in cream, not realizing country
power, came innocent to everything.
Stopped reading, music, tried the cards,
dressed dolls, sawdust tarts that sprawled on beds
for charity, and in three days had a child
that would ride a tricycle full tilt
into the special wallpaper of the claustrophobia.

Married, I escaped, yet I would pace
my guilt with my children across half a continent
to wheel onto the neglected gravel at five o'clock
precisely (twelve hours from Painesville)
beside the thin hibiscus–they never would give
that tropical bloom: thrown-up peanuts
on the back seat, crayons everywhere, and the recent
headache from tunnels on the Pike and vapor lock,
and the thousands of paper napkins and happy stories:
there she would be,

sitting in the swing, waiting,
and he, of course, late at the office.

Oh, she could be awful. Made the son
sit in a straight chair when he did not want to,
"An exercise in discipline," looked at a drawing
of a covered wagon and two horses (I knew), sneered,
"Is that the best you can do?"
I could have killed her then; but when the two
were old enough to learn dominoes and she taught
them at the kitchen table but kept pushing
the black-and-white tabs into perfect place, I decided
There's no earthly use. In fact, they enjoyed it.

I woke suddenly.
Silent as she stepped (the attic door, for she slept
up there now, left open for the flow of air)
and purposeful as silence, I awoke, heart
alert and eyes, my pupils, staring, listening.
The little girl
slept in the cot next my bed. She came and lowered,
a dim shape in her modest nightgown, over the cot.
She could have had a razor, or removed,
so gently, the mortal pillow from under the small head.
I saw the two figures, one bodily
echo of my own, and the other, bending.
No need to think of breathing.
What she did
was to lift a single strand
of limp warm hair from that head, take it into her hand
and stroke it so lightly that a bird

would not wake.
I heard the sigh, piteous, pitying,
and the dawn-wind words: "Ah, the pretty,
oh, the poor pretty thing."
I could have loved her, then,
had I not been coward there, and since.
Pretty. Poor pretty thing.

Time, and times. And my tall, now,
for her age
daughter says, as I come down
another staircase
from another day's
stress as from a wooden platform
erected permanently behind the eyes of my mind,
"I like the way you always change
your dress before supper"; I don't wince
unless it is to smile; and we both watch
for the car turning in to the drive.

HOMAGE TO ROBERT LOWELL

i

Like you, I have come home to these high hills
and this low river, salt-bound and fettered;
I sense people shuttered in these clapboard houses
standing at bay's edge, that mere gap in ocean,
figureheads behind curtains starched like foam,
scrimshaw folks.
            How beautiful the fall is here!
Tough grass and tumbled stone
walls merciful to small creatures
looking to winter's crannies (one winter here
is worth a dozen out-of-state) out of the wind.
Gulls turn on autumn's wheel, we are all
gulls no matter what season,
but some are more nobly gulled than others.

ii

Who is to tell
who is to say
Old Puritan
what's to be done
to wit to who
who'll sing
who'll dance
we wish to what
whisht the word
to sin
let's bend
our hinges crook our pins
queer the changes
rest a while
us gulls
scoff but deliver

iii

Sin   sin   sin   salt   sin

iv

Man with the long twig on his tree
is buttoned up from less to more
and only breathes his branches when
his used wife sleeps and he can lie
at length dreaming of his final whore.
But we were all of us green once.
Once we all whirled our pines
on that sublime, monotonous shore.

v

How can I say you are bound
to be Prometheus, or even
unbound, when you are the rock?
Your wound festers, though.
Rub salt. Drink vinegar.
Suffer. Suffer.
High up beaks circle on great wings.
Your iron eyes
draw them. Chained, you will grow
viridian like inland statutes.
Your relatives in tennis shoes
will come to hang
a wreath on your barnacles.
In winter your moss beard
will howl green into the north
by northeast wind.

vi

Your new widow walks
the icy path you built

on the top of your square house.
Only the iron rail
keeps her from tumbling over.
They say you've sent her mad with rhyme.
Walks, walks, and does not look down.
She has grown more thin, she has grown more tall,
she is not the woman you knew,
she cannot know you now,
that she did she will not allow.
She is thin as glass, tall as frost,
self-willed as a ghost.

While you sat brown in your study,
relying on metaphors (pen, ink, paper, the motion
of an arm across an artificial horizon),
did she plan her roof-rise?
You had your muse.
When you first saw her, by the gate
into the August field, she turned on you
and your green, your burning
her bruised blue gaze
like holes in ice
on a bright cold day.
So marred, you married her by God,
begot, and the steeple shook
the main part of the sky.

Motionless on the lawn down there
that paradigm of dark New England nun,
the solitary elm,
elegant, watchful, and withdrawn,
sinks aged roots deep in the bitter snow.

But you indoors were tortured by your trust
and summer visions of the swan
your father took you on, no common swan
but godling's toy and carrying
garden varieties of Ledas leaning to leaving sailors
ignorant of Zeus and certain family
connections, and you, always the youngest,
always anguished and the most vulnerable,
charming and serious in your Seabee suit.

vii

Didn't you like
come on now
didn't you just enjoy
that mad being prisoned
the grating like rhyme
like solid metre
you knew where you were
where you were you were new
and you wanted to sing
in your little Bedlam
in your little yard wide
so you sang and you graphed
and the walls ran true?
Didn't you?
Oh you conscious
objector! Sprung
you ran free
you sprang free
you staggered,

you
our skunk hour, striped with tar
and whitewash, towards
and through the marble arch
old, on the march,
the old poet-animal
we admire, we applaud
but we cannot emulate
that wave of your inkstained paw
as you pass with your age,
your weapon
your intact, virtuous reason.
Maybe you are the good badger
and maybe
we have got our myths mixed.

viii

But you shed muses and disguises like worn wings.
You travel, scouting compass clipped

to a sad black sock. No wonder
rain slicks Paris, you bring your weather with you.
Cluny, the Louvre, 'Dame, the same
hotel door revolving.
Berlin is even better: dirty mist
under the lindens haloes Loreleis.
Prose can be sometimes helpful. You can drown
your lineal sorrows in that eau-de-vie,
but wait for the real thing
the filthy-aproned servant with the leer
and bandy legs brings in: the beer
brown as the Kavanaugh at home.
That's where your needle quivers to—
confess, in Rome, that Michelangelo can go
from Newton to Dorchester on the cars
and sketch that stretching finger, Adam's, out to God.
A sacrament may be contained
in that small box whereof the smell
is Gorton's Codfish Cakes; Portugee wine
grace a chalice. In the name of Him Who died: Amen,
for Christ's (New England) sake.

ix

Wander your beaches
strewn with November grammar of your heart.
Your little hound
follows your heelprints, his tail a quill
between arthritic haunches:
brush-cut, he quivers with his stubborn faith.
You turn away from January questions,
only a fool would venture that far north,
but your dog comes on. You miss a priest, but he
knows the odor of your overcoat.

x

I stand at the end of the pier.
It is winter for many of us; or near.

Have you gone in? Are you working, in the cottage,
on your translations, posing chariots
on the swells near Samoset? What of Chaucer?
Looking down from the end of the pier,
not speaking for others, I see
green moving slime, ice floes, old men
their furled umbrellas wrapped in kelp
heaving like flails, coiling like life,
declaiming bile-green nouns in their galoshes.
Behind the underwater Child's streaked windows,
mermaids clash quahog shells like cymbals.
If we look back to the still shore
on that still shore the granite
rock leads light into itself.

THE OLD PEOPLE TAKE TO THE SKY

Out of my element
I like a slangy phrase, it makes me feel,
although I know I'm not,
a bit more easy in my mind. Therefore,
we got our traps out early, pulled our boots
on, and here we are! Strapped in the leather
belly bands, what horses we are riding—I recall
how as a girl I'd take the gates at nooning on my way
to the men in the field with a pie in one hand and the water-
pail in the other and not spill a drop—
in the shifting
queer track of our going to seek
what Son said, the lineaments of space. Or some such notion.
Before it's too late, he meant. We did not take
offense. That boy's in love with air.

It's a little plane, a gray like my old Bess
but livelier, quicker,
with those dials.
We gathered our legs beneath us, and jumped off!
Son's wrist is sure, he would have made
a good horseman.
I like a saddle better than these seats.

You needn't think because of what
I've said we're pure
Yankee Gothic. Because we haven't flown before
it doesn't follow that we don't know Greek.
We get into Boston, see a show,
I put my hair up in the Psyche knot,
we dine at Marliave's after a turn
about the graveyard, get home safe by midnight—
the Airflow's a reliable machine.

My husband's a decliner from way back.
Look at him, he's distinguishable,
his white fine hair, his vanity, his long
drawn bones. Hands perched on knees,
he translates through his thinning veins
the current force that guides us to the depths
of height as though he's listening to high
Greek twitterings of wire-swinging birds.

Sitting on the porch, with binoculars . . .
sea-birds, mostly. Circling in a slow
slash of sky, Son brings our island close.
The house we live in down there clings
a speck, a wart, a limpet
that small to its rock. My garden!
Zinnias, cockscomb, dahlias, hardy flowers
raked up from scrabbled soil—that was work,
that little crabbed hooked rug
of brightness for the hearth of day.
(We damped the fire just before we left.)
Three bean-pole teepees, the blue roof:
toys, toys. I think of the rows of indoor books
and of how I have dusted them and their damp
spotted leaves and shaken
ancient letters, shag and burnt
matchmarkers out of them for years.
Benignant diseases! How on earth
did we come to settle, you may ask,
I'm asking, for such terms? Up here we rock in air,
but our hut shudders shingled by the wind
that warps the cedar as it whistles through
gaps in my vision

that widen, that is deflected by the sight
of the coarse blue dollops of ocean ladled out
to the mouths of uncountable rivers—
what do our shallop's oars,
our parasols and cushions have to do
with that live fathomless assault on our threescore ten?
Only, our instincts own
more property than we guessed.

We are hazarding. Our dowser's hand
clips firmly to his stick. Our noontime Charon.
If this is dying, I am for it.
He has flown in war, he has dropped death
who argued for the splinted wing
for the wounded gull. Are we his good burdens?
The word comes, "We are over Galilee."
I recognize the village as I see
him falling like a cross, he is stretching
in flames his hand toward me
and I am falling, falling–

No, no, I am not ill, I am perfectly
in ascension. That's not right.
But I am.
My body is ascending on its metal wings
to where the sky dissolves
in enormous rings out from the sun.

His lighted head lifts, he leans back hard
on his wand. Power is in him, we are in his power.
My eyes expand like grains
brought up to what is blazing day,
day springing. Yes, I remember,
but I have not thought of it for
so many seasons of my skin
how we flew, we spun, twin compasses
fixed to that single spire,
how I never once considered
falling and what a far way
and the prayer for the drowning, all that is drowned
in my smile that is all-
seeing, filling my ears with sweet breath
as I sprint straight ahead in my glistening
breastplate of silver
along the true line he has drawn for us
simply between two transfigurations,
those he has saved for us,
half-turning in his deathseat
and winking immensely across at his father.

I am temporarily
put down, I bend to my duty to wring
the neck of the thermos and pour the oblation,
while the whole time I am running beyond
in my being. I know the signs, let them talk
as they will of Pegasus
who with his sharpened hoof struck Helicon's
steep side and freed the sacred well;
of Phaethon, even Apollo's son, whose fiery steeds
provided loving cause for his demise:
from waxen shrouds I unwrap sandwiches.
Our picnic in his sky. When as a child
I learned the sky was not a roof,
not solid, and not really blue, I wept.
Hated the fact-teller worse than learning
of the curse, or sex. Under the blue
umbrella of my ignorance, those seemed natural.
Take that away,
who could tell what might get in?
Now in the middle of our old
age, we glance at each other shy, as though
we're newly young. If I should speak,
what language would he hear?

Listen. A shadow nears that is not fair.
We enter, or it enters us, the real cloud this time
that bursts stinging
seeds around our gray flower, and get
the glimpse of the savage
storm-swimmer, mouth bawling hail, hurtling past us
into the heart of the thunderfall,
and pull back fearful from the isinglass
and the evidence that he is
out there forever, the other swimmer of the hour,
a-gape, in agony, and gasping for the net,
a reeling of compassion, or a gaff
(I've seen them speared;
what entrails he must have). Repent,
repent in time you can escape!
I am pressing my hands together in a vessel
tipped to the sun whose saviour rays

betray him and endow
our bark with threads that carry
our frail keen ark to what could be
the fin of a violent mountain
we crowd upon but coast past,
so much is past, the new
is only old turned out to light:
and I did love you once, you old,
old man.

We are over the giant's shield of hammered gold,
the giant is sleeping; on his breathing breast
those insects of the sea,
the fishing boats, are going home.
It is ours, the field of the cloth of gold,
and we croon above its greasy fleece,
not forgetting crowned, encrusted deities
who stayed their final shafts, and stain
its moving surfaces with benevolent gleam.
Legends. The sun is sinking, or we are.
Yet we are being guided, yet we are ordering
our fall. We shall lose
Artemis as we come
having bested the sun to rising dark,
tiredly, to the horizon of so much grace.
Cease the vibration. I am weary, I confess.
In a splendid ordinary gesture
he takes his spectacles off, folds them
to a frown he tucks in his pocket.
Open the door, step down. Let's wait for him,
he still has things to do. I trust him, though.
He will catch up with us.

Arm in arm, so,
let us go to the terminal. Someone else, I suppose,
will stable the fabulous,
give it the decent feed that it deserves.
Maybe it will stand trembling a while,
the feel of splintered elements in its metal skin.
I somehow feel it kin. It's small,

and homely, after all.
The actual event is always simple.
I know I am.
Later, in my disguise of stars,
I'll make the old men Bovril, laced with gall.

THE OLD HOUSE

Ivy swings inward at the window,
Three wasps crawl upon the pane,
Elderly wasps and older ivy.
Ivy is fancy, wasps are plain.

Here lived the beautiful Hotchkiss sisters:
Laura, Eulalia, and Emily Jane.
Once they were courted by half the county
(Ivy is fancy, wasps are plain).

Once they were courted by half the county,
carriages thronging the riverbent lane,
Tall young men with presents and prospects
(Three wasps buzz upon the pane).

Father remarked of the frequent proposals
To Laura, Eulalia, and Emily Jane
(Father was rich and Mama was poorly),
"Somebody's loss is somebody's gain."

(Ivy swings inward at the window.)
Daughters are daughters, and love is vain.
Here live the elderly Hotchkiss sisters.
Three wasps buzz upon the pane.

THE LOST BOY

His photograph got in
with the family others. Nobody recognizes
him, not even the everybody's mother.
S. T. Wiggins, Ground Floor Gallery, No. 15
Commercial Street, Cedar Rapids, Iowa
is what's printed on
the back of the evidence.
Oh, the careful combing of his hair!
Two years old probably, he retains
his Buddha look, inscrutable, hinting at worlds.
Exquisite listening ear,
adze nose, his mouth judgemental, remarkable
in one so young; in a dress and sash.
A single booted foot protrudes beneath the hem.
Its angle I could kiss with reverence.
The fingers of the tiny hands dispose
themselves politically upon the fierce
upholstered arms of the chair that suffers
them, ending in tired lion's claws.
He has a power.
More than statesman, not much less
than transplanted god,
such a passenger
sits, a good baby, for the lens.
I should say before the First World War.
I told you, worlds ago. He does not whimper
or dwindle. He has disappeared from our mirrors
that he might have inherited: no,
he comes because he is gone,
having chosen perhaps to go with that clear
intimidating gaze
to lisp at Plato's knees, from Emerson
and Thoreau, Hawthorne among the sycamores.
Hedges of Osage oranges
stand between him and them. Nevertheless,
Negatives available for future orders.

THREE AND ONE, ARROWMOOSIC

Too cold to swim.
June, too. We might have known.
Let's play a game.
What kind of games
you girls know how to play?
Euchre.
Hearts.
What's that game
we played in the car coming down?
The one you play by yourself?
Only game I really know how to play is euchre.
Poker?
Deuces wild.
Larry, you would say that.
Honestly, Larry, you're a scream.
Linda, you deal. You're kidding! Me?
(Curlers aglow, she deals.)
Juanita's got two kings. Juanita,
I can see your hand.
You can see my hand?
They got us beat already. Larry,
I bet you got an ace over there
you use every time.
Let's bury somebody.
Larry, let's bury Larry.
Sharon, get some water.
Don't get it in my hair.
Put your arms down by your sides,
we got to lay you out.
Don't kick it at me, chrissake.
His toes are impossible!
You didn't do
a very good job, sister, I don't think
you know what you're doing,
tell you the truth.
Linda, hold his ankles.
Sharon brings water in her cap. He pretends
terror. They must touch him. Ritual. Hey!

He resurrects,
brushes sand
like flies off his torso, legs
apart
tolerant
fully operative
(Shoot,
I'm going in).

RECURRENT

Always the same house.
Sunk deep in summer, shingled by the salt,
rambling like ancestors to the young,
crumbling, wind-woven, gull-hovered,
their cries like ours as children,
questions: "Who's there?" "How's that?"
Always the voices.

Ghosts and sea airs, the day's dreck
strewn on the stairs, damp towels, the sand–
"Bring in the whole outdoors!"
The parlor's wrecked melodeon
keys fallen yellow
petals to the verdigris;
Shakespeare on the bookshelf growing pearls.

One arm of the wicker chair
loose as an elbow–
"Of course he always liked his drop."
Uncle Captain that would be,
played his part in the mutiny,
sleeps northeast in his pegleg bed,
dies with his glass eye in its cup

The jilted cousin walks
a mermaid on knives, carries her headache
a bridal wreath to the sea wall
where a malingering
parasol lies like a shot bird.
On the lawn collapsed a canvas wrack; untranslated,
the novel abandoned to the wet grass.

Sea-fern light in upper rooms,
bureau drawers nervous with unmatched gloves.
"Which did she marry? I never got that straight."
"Ah, but she had the second sight."
So they pursue past time recurrent as dreams.
'The green bird sings in the coral tree':
Lorelei, Lorelei. Chanted, I pace that strand,
bound by a grandmother's fine gold chains.

EASTER IN NEW ENGLAND

i

The Caretaker

So often I come home
by the back way across the lower field
and through the smaller wood
the path is plain now under melting snow
sometimes the sunset through the leaf-
reft ranks of beech and birch
so this day whistling soft
because of the mild and noticing
tracks nothing much the usual
deer fox Henderson's dog–
I was brought up short by the sight
no hawk's mouse weasel's kill I know them
neighbors on the hill
and there was cloth mixed in
I put my axe down hunkered sniffed
stood up and looked around
I tried to think the thing out clear
did rabbit squeal and snake dive under
did a voice whisper and I not aware
raise high your homely weapon
bring it down again raise
bring down how many times
did the voice cry out
Someone must live
at evensong how far that bell
sounds from the village
nearer the owl's cold question

ii

The Recluse

I live here alone one room
in the decaying mansion

my friends wild creatures crows'
quills witchgrass certain stones
speak to me dry herbs in season
trim my own wicks put in chinks
against the windflute's stops
winter charms nevertheless
I fear the waterlight of dreams
imagine a light form moving there
subtle elusive as water
how long ago
the clock ticks loud enough to bury thought
I live here alone I will live here
alone I latch my door
take up the lamp and climb
step by reluctant step the stair
beside my hunching shadow on the wall
that echoes my true burden not at all
that meets me at the turning of the hall
my nightly passage empty chambers making sure
my dwelling's mine alone
and I my only ghost both guest and host

iii

The Carpenter

Just your luck I heard you knock
that bell don't ring
I happened to be working in the hall
hammering nails in these old houses
pop out like sins in Sunday school
but walk in mind the bitch
she'll get between your legs
you don't look like you want a coffin yet
that's just my joke my stock in trade
come haven't you to view
my treasures I can tell you now
my mourning scenes are not for sale
although you antique yearners don't give up
easy up here and mind your footing

that tread's loose again
my hammer's handy if the need arise
follow me and I'll raise the blind
for your edification gaze
to your heart's disease the light falls best
from this north window excuse the dust
living the way I do
I'm garrulous such company
as I'm used to being lately dead
most of my family had black hair
miles of it in these pictures
hair stitched on linen you'll observe
these subjects are well known
wreaths urns tombs willows weeping females
(I own a fondness for the Magdalene)
enough grief to turn a windmill
often I cry out loud
at them gone under and me tramping earth
I don't suppose you'll know the name
the matter constituting any frame
wood's as I said my livelihood
I find coffins simple and steady
couple a week in a green winter
but for the frames I opt for bone
Just run your thumb along one side
feel how smooth feel how cold
where wood's alive porous natural
left to itself it rots of course
but in the rotting's warm
in the final stages throws off light
I wonder at the knife could curve
these into warpful ornament
you say you've an appointment somewhere else
we'll go on down take care or stop
I'll go down first don't think you've lost
you've seen the pictures they'll come back
some dream I don't dream much
but when I wake I'm thankful
keep straight on the path
to the churchyard you can't miss
the lychgate's at the end
until next visit friend

iv

The Witness

When at dawn the red deer delicately approach the pond
to drink in the cold water-transfigured light
at my kitchen basin washing off the night
I think of the murderer
washing and washing his hands
in the rosy brackish pool of that other sun
and of the mother anxious for no reason
twisting her hands in her apron while the supper cools
how at the very instant she cried out blindly
how when they brought him at last
she progressed calmly to meet them although
their footsteps had mutilated early her irises

v

The Visitor

When you entered at first
the light was behind you
filling the doorway the arrowy sky
as you advanced
into my low-ceilinged room
I saw that your arms were laden with flowers
offerings which you heaped on my speechless table
you left as you had come
without identifying yourself
I understood I was forgiven
my hands fell silent as leaves
my shoulders carried a drift of snow

vi

The Recusant

Sunday morning and the bell
the sweet wound of sound the steeple visible
floating in thin blue mist
like a strangler's scarf at God's
white gloriously vulnerable throat
Did you hear the owl last night? The call

prickling the buds of the lilac?
Lilies reproach the sepulchre
a phantom flock bleats in the chancel
for a shepherd or a judge and find to feed
their redemptive hunger their poor thirst
only the gentle stupor of the Lamb
the ritual cannot suffice my parable
is solitary and must stand
and sing its throat cut
bleeding in a bush
in my new miracle water is altered wine
colorless clean and cold in the cup of stone
incorruptible
Father can you recall my name?
Once I stood with the others
sang Father Son Holy Ghost we sprang up gladly
but it was not my place
I could not make my peace
forgive me not for I know what I do
in sight of unstained windows
force you up to where you will not beg
to where you'll die first
cruelty's my friend
lover playfellow heart's companion truly
I lie down with it rise up with it
and may die of its embrace—
what deaths we puritans
put each other to
while the hymn rages you shall not utter
I have you I shall have you
young strong replete resplendent
a great wave torrent flood
behold I rush upon you
unblemished undiminished it is you
a city reared on the plain
a fortress walled by stars
it is you I would resurrect
God Lazarus out of my slaying furious
we grapple across our open graves

THE LEAF RAKERS

Summer magnificence of those other lives!
Leaning on marble
parapets, treading mosaic
terraces, strolling meticulous
lawns of particular green,
always in hearing of music
or fountains, always with unobstructed
views of the sea
rumpled like blue real linen,
yacht sails correctly upright
each in its glass of air.
Over multiflorescence of roses
the sun pours gold.
Those other people speak so fluently
the language of leisure;
when they walk briskly, they perambulate,
meander,
take a cliff ramble. If there is dancing,
they float to mirrors. Swimming,
they seldom drown.
Only the child of one palazzo,
Boadicea of the pony cart,
crinkled hair, fluted skirts streaming,
legs braced apart stands and whips whips whips
her sheltie up and down Bellevue
furious afternoons.
Those people clip their coupons like birds' wings.
Ah, portescocheres and the pleasures of
portmanteaus, parquetry, portieres, coquetry
among the hydrangeas–passementerie!
Reticuled, corseted, Laliqued,
leg-o'-muttoned, vested, flocked, gold-chained
under basrelief gold leaf loggia ceilings
they perform
the passacaglia of their peacock days.
Autumn, they take passage south.

Now the leaf rakers come.
Wrinkled as elm, tough as maple
leaves they travel the grounds,
ray out over gold-stricken lawns,
drift from gravel drives onto cooling stone
of bereft terraces,
cleave
to terra cotta urns and the thinning vines
of trailing geraniums, shrivelled,
their long stems
attached to yellow-gloved fingers,
fanned bamboo combs
primed to catch phantoms.
They bring their own
baskets, used years,
bursting out at dreams.
Their native language is smoke.
They never look at the sea
(this season deepest blue
of the paper the linenmaids have rolled
the white fifty tablecloths in)
but work work rake brown
terriculous eyes gold bent,
backs like scythe handles
harvesting themselves.
On a weather breeder
they gather plunder of emptied baskets
into great heaps of tarnished tender,
set the matches in.
Burning gold in windless air
strokes straight up towards the hurricane.

THE BLUE UMBRELLA

To extend one's circle and to change
the color of the field of one's shadow
is always pleasant and the blue
umbrella is enjoying this afternoon
doing just that set to dry on the tarry
black floor of the barn after the rain
the sun shining through the barn window
widens its sphere of influence
turning that new sky blue

DISJUNCTIVE

Your days go more quickly than ours.
Here in the 3 a.m. dark
we grow restless because of the daylight
greeting of doves in your dooryard.
The clink of your breakfast spoons
as they round the teacups disturbs us,
also the brightness of the marmalade.
When we rise rumpled from bed
you have already gone on the river,
one of you leisurely poling the punt,
the other, the Cornish-haired girl,
trailing her hand in the water.
As the warmth recedes from the meadows
and a late thrush sings in the wood,
noon strides into our field.
At our supper, you fall asleep.
Our midnights don't mingle, our dreams
hang separate as planets.
When you touch down again on our tarmac
our meeting will turn back,
turn forward the intimate clock.

MEMENTO

Aunt Eva came that year across the lake
from Toronto on the steamer: she was big,
full-breasted, almost six feet tall.
She wore a blue suit and a white crepe blouse
with a jabot. She was coming home.

Dark, bulky, imperious
with the family charm, she brought legends:
singing in her sleep after voice lessons,
divorce, the second-floor suicide door
she nearly walked out of – she brought me
a necklace of forget-me-nots,

blue and white small beads
knotted tightly with no space between.
'Here we are,' she said, resonant, clasping
her gift round my nine-year-old neck.
I never knew why, then, there, so immediate
with the car waiting.
The back of the steamer was churning.

Next summer she was down
to a skeleton. One Sunday morning
in her red bathrobe in the Port house
as I was playing Grieg's 'Butterfly' on the upright,
she leaned on the parlor door-frame
her hand a yellow leaf on the polished wood.
When I had finished, she said from a hollow,
'Don't let them stop you. Don't forget.'

FOR FRIENDS, ON THE BIRTH OF REBECCA

Make all you can of beauty quickly.
The rush in the blood, the heightening
blush to the cheek of the lovely –
take measure of these, and advantage:
look at topography and time in this new face,
remark indent of valley, sweet dusky swell
of hills above milky lakes
(morning mist). Do not dwell
on vacancies of this landscape
but imagine a music for reeds, music toneless and lunar;
before it fades, recall the radiance of
other geographies in other spheres.
If you must turn away at last,
gaze deep here first at least.

MARUSHKA

First the big Outer One
the Entertainer-Container,
barrel-shaped, painted in primary
colors, top of her blue, skirt red,
face painted in on her wooden head—
two blackbirds flying, Morse code eyes, smile
two red parts of a second grade heart.
How she sings, dances, envelops!

Crack her in her middle,
twist open and out pops a sister
smaller and smarter, short-sighted,
starched, wasp-waisted, governess,
stewardess on the Atlantic run.
Be wary, she's lively, you'll inherit
that gold watch, those pince-nez.

The mad sister's thinner still.
A fog-white frill
flutters her throat.
The second sails on,
but her eyes are smudged
horizons she doesn't know.
Be careful with her,
she has a gift for you.

Then the grandmother, little Babushka. She
should have been first
but the All-Encompassing
took over, they always do,
said Get out of the way,
said Get into me,
I'm having you.

And you:
you're the last,
the pink baby,

sweet size of the
tiniest finger,
the most delicious
mouthful, Marushka.

NIGHTSHADES

I am your childhood governess, demure
in dove gray and chain and locket;
chalk like my minatory finger
scrapes the soft blackboard of your dreams.

I am also your nurse on the midnight shift,
inserting my silvery icicle, my mercurial rod –
how your fever hangs on,
your hot, dry verities.

Again, I am your little seamstress,
my needle pulling, my thimble pushing
the thread of your lifelong monody.
Not my skin I prick.

Then I am your good hausfrau
smelling of apples, yeasty, reliable,
polishing your knobs and frames, shining
vanity's oval eye.

I am your Scheherezade, in my silk trousers
cross-legged with my lute in the window-seat.
While you take your ease on my peacock cushions,
what lies I tell!

THE PET

O say see
look at my lit
tle monkey
she so puzzled and charming
with that almost human frown

she sits in her lit
tle chair
at her little table
she holds a pen
she is writing

making strange
marks on the white
petalled paper
I am very proud
of her

she is coming
along very nicely
but sometimes
chatters more
than I prefer

and would tear up the page
chew it to bits
did I not interfere
always calmly and stroke
her down

THE TOY TOTEM

Lucia, lacking, daughter
of Joy, see James your father
leaning on his nib
making tracks
across the blank page of the room
(Paris, maybe, or Trieste, triste,
the furnishings
the same, only the smells and colors change,
the paper is always narcissus).
Your eyes are like dark plums,
they do not reflect.
Turn away, turn,
and set your bulbous brow against the pane
to hear *da capo* the sweet careless tenor
of the rain. 'Her mind
is brilliant, marvel of clairvoyance,'
he, your singing feather-father, said of you.
Pity you cannot read.
Yet why should you? The reign
of words is meaningless not sensed
as a paroxysm of leaves
whirled to the upper storey
to circle, a convulsion of green doves,
a wreath of arrows, light, Lucia,
making your translation-dream
weightless and speaking
from your half-born brain,
informing those dead-end streets
your eyes; winding laurel
affliction a true blessing
among your coarse and unbound hair.
Lean, then, lean your wreathed brow
towards the wellspring of the rain
that you may speak with thick-tongued flowers.

CAMOFLEUR

Some women's power
resides in the elbow
sharp as a cat's or curved
a cradle.
Some, in the nostrils' flare
the set of the mouth
the meekness of earlobes.
That night in the rented villa
when you washed your hair in the bath
and came out turbanned to the sitting-room
I saw for the first time your eyebrows
the Brooklyn Bridge Fourth of July
radium Halley's Comet Revelation
a curtain lifted – next day as usual
we walked on cliffs above the sea.

IN THE TENT

At night words crouch outside like Bedouins
waiting to wreck our silence
we have pitched in this desert
that so becomes our lives
hung about with the comforts of not speaking,
the exotic rugs, the cots,
the books we have carried with us:
guardians of the threshold through which speech
would pour with its scimitars,
its murderous weapons, its curved knives.

SUBSISTENCE LEVEL

It is in a marginal land that subsistence is possible.
Find me water, bring it in your hands,
expect some spilling and go back
a thousand times to the fortunate spring:
I've selected
pebbles and grasses for the soup.
Now make me fire, rub and rub,
I'll breathe and we'll be warm.
Thankful for remnants, stones, weeds, breath.
Contaminated as they are!
                                                  The satellites
are bright tonight. Although I miss the stars
the bloody sun will rise with its familiar dust
at what we are accustomed to call dawn.

It is in a marginal land
one reads the old book of the mind,
the pages stained, the print blurred,
the title torn away and the spine bitten,
slurring the evidence fitfully yet stubborn
with irritation at the lapses
of memory, the withering of cells.
Twig for pencil, one marks for a while
certain phrases that have a turn;
and when the twig wears out, the fingernail
grows with a life of its own.
Love. Not fair. And, where did we go wrong?
We are left with our bodies and our will,
and the sky which, after the firestorm, may fail.

After the grass, the roots. The dirt last.
If you die,
I have no shovel.
                                    Condors, take care.
You see I know your name. You have an enemy below
before my eyes become clear glass
through which reflections and their objects pass
without trace, filtered by liquid and by air

till eyes and objects disappear
along with our picked bones
(the flesh consumed since that we called
beautiful, and we were right). Care, take care,
'A stone look on a stone's face.'
Yet when my love comes walking
towards me on his ghostly sticks
I shall recognize his insect guise,

his gaze like staring lozenges
bent upon wires, and his elegant, imploring glance,
I shall leave off eating earth and raise
myself on the widow of an elbow,
feel it resolve, absolved to wing
like cloud, veined, and sized
to match his own. My abdomen folds in,
I put out legs for extra antennae, my vision's
cut to facets, my brain shrinks
to the head of a pin. Even though the sun
remain poised a moment more before the final plunge,
we shall have cast off for the flight
and, coupled, indissoluble, entered the world.
At sunset, the wind dropped, and it was possible
to begin to assess the extent of the destruction.

THE FIND

Those that have eyes like oysters, let them close
their valves. They would not listen anyhow

to the worldwide ravaged breathing of the sea
that turns over and over in its salt-infested lungs

the great conundrum gone to wrack and rubble,
the continuous pebble death-rattle

making for them their stuccoed shells
bungalows on the developer's ocean floor

that protect such really suburban natural
depravity beneath each calcified little roof

as well as the glister one of them may produce
by the illness walking men call chance –

imagine: a million oysters opening their lids
and exhaling, Take me! My submarinal life revealed

and my accretionary habits,
my pipe and slippers, my making love to a piece of grit

night after Saturday night, with this gem
of time burning in my pale indoors forehead

unnoticed, needing no adorning, unspeakable.
Yet I know the tides above me, how they turn,

and the poor fisherman, barefoot on the shingle
each dawn, in the opaline mist,

who is ready to wade and bleed into the sharp shallows
as he bends his whole skinny body towards

the direction of his starving sight
that has behind it five wormy children and the hut

with the torn rotogravure of his empirical Sovereign
pinned to the bamboo wall by a white fishbone

like his hand when he grasps and pries from me
his fortune with the grain of sand,

the tiny irritant, the fate or cyst
on which our visions were impaled and grew.

OBJECTS OF VISION

I

I am in the mirror
my image is in the mirror
my two eyes thus
my nose my mouth I imagine
my image in the mirror
except for the mark the blemish
where I have placed
my finger on my lips

hush! my mind is in the dark
conspiring
at the back of the silver
listening waiting
as though behind a window shutter
for the crowds that pass in the street
for the one figure to detach itself
and come forward to the glass

II

In the country of the tree
the single leaf that falls
is of course the tree
falling from itself

and the stone already lichened
in the field of the tree
the hieroglyph of the leaf
can change the meaning of

III

Leaning over the edge
looking down into the well
one sees an eye
magnified by water

surrounded by stone
one's eye reflected
a welling of darkness
one could drown in that eye

IV

A leaf fallen and floating
on the surface of the water
a note on a mirror
an idea from outside

V

On the stone fronts of the many houses
the damp has made vital impressions
as of hands of the blind
feeling their way to the market
to the bazaars
most of the windows are shuttered
behind them one senses an eye
appliqued to the blind
waiting for the refraction
of light on the oblique
in the darkness of living rooms
the white caps of housewives quiver
the tree-patterned paper puts down roots
the grandfather taps with his cane
as he climbs the stair to the attic
where at night the moon shines in
he crosses on his way
to the window and the telescope
the moon tonight is full he hunches to
she leaps to his watery eye
beset with stars in his dotage
in his excitement he reads
the cloud passing over her countenance
as a letter from a rival
an idea from outside

VI

An old man with his eye pressed to an image within
a brain overgrown with patterns like a stone in
a field
an aged grasshopper in a green frock coat
an old opera-goer
(having hung up his cloak and cane)
still I am drawn to him
his gaze on my craters
his daughter endures him
his son-in-law despises him
if a child laughs he weeps
for the end of laughter
for him I could preen shall become
all round and silver forthwith for this miser
hoarder of my sensational coin
how he would lie about me how he would like
to slide me under his mattress
take me out polish me during his daily siesta
his windfall his dearest
put me a monocle to his memories
I slide away from his lens up the sky
an idea an image he a cloud
passing over my countenance
a mote on a mirror
a leaf on the surface
changing the meaning of

THE IMAGE

Two lines more
on my forehead that were not there
this time last year

Soon I may wear
long sleeves and arrange
the ritual bronze chrysanthemums
in the blue-glazed pottery jar

Remembering
the opening of my country –
how we bowed to the strange fair men
who stepped from their rough-sailed vessels
fresh from the glittering sea

Again perhaps
my gauze-shrouded image
will be moved under cover of night
to the tenth-month new shrine

TO A PATRON

I vary in my health towards douce
and may yet be permitted to walk out
among the great numbers of unburied dead.
There'll be a statue of me yet,
plaster because of lack of blood.
In all seriousness, I am in a deuce of a hole.
Too ill to go to church,
although I daresay I'll arrive in time,
before my true self has caught up
with the course. Do not, do not
crush the winged slippers of Mercury.
But my own prayer is to survive the talons
or at least elude just long enough
to create your bronze doors –
will they close on that?

OFF THE BEATEN TRACK

'What is a mind?' – Elizabeth Pliskoff

I

The valley is hung about with mountains
the mountains are hung with clouds
the glacier cuts through
the south face of the nearest mountain

In the valley's safe hollow
the houses cluster like cells
the village is like a hive
every morning
the workers fly out to their tasks
some with brooms some with baskets
some with axes others with rakes

In the houses women ply
back and forth back and forth –
bread rises under damp linen cloths
wash coils in steaming copper vessels
the loom overhead
stamps like a horse!

In the doorway of a shed
at the rear of one of the houses
a spider is spinning its web
in this shed unused machinery
sits garnering rust
but the spider is not idle either
out on the meadow sheep crop
lichens act on stones
Tink! Tank! Time to move on

II

The glacier cuts slowly

III

At noon in the communal hall
occurs a great clanking as of grounded bells
on the heavy scrubbed tables
the men
their cheeks seamed with chaff
their eyebrows like ledges
their eyes like rocks tossed up by the plow
have come in from the fields
behind them
the women hoist brimming pitchers
from which at a signal they pour
into the tankards the fresh ruddy liquid
the harvested fountain of trees
the young girls
pliant as birches in their white aprons
their hair parted like ripe wheat sheaves
bear the heaped platters into the hall
under the noisy rafters
the eaters spear the yield

IV

During this time
the sky remains cloudless
the glacier shines like a plate

V

In mid-afternoon
a group of climbers appears in the village
but seeing the houses shuttered
the street (as they think) deserted
they shrug and trudge off with their packs
this was not the right place

VI

A pair of shutters is opened
a woman leans out and smiles
dreamily over the valley

a slight exhalation from the glacier
lengthens the shadows of the pines

Moments later
an old woman rushes from a cottage
she throws her black shawl over her head
and rocks back and forth
in the middle of the street
wailing

VII

One day snow flies along the track
where the climbers disappeared
at sunset a rosy light
enters the western sector
icicles bar the windows
of houses whose mounded roofs
over the one warm room
shelter children being fed from wooden bowls
in the chimney corner the grandmother
sits with her needles knitting
the brown woolen stocking for the youngest
the one with round eyes
who watches the shape of the stocking
growing like Italy!
In the same room
the mother become stout
scours the bowls and returns them
to their place in a row on the mantel
the spoons she nests in a drawer which she closes
the father is carving in wood by the fire
he hopes to lure many doves
in the spring migration

VIII

Crouched in the windowseat
the daughter wets a finger
and reads on fiercely

The moon rises smoothly over the glacier
as a cat rinses its fur

IX

In a dwelling set apart
set on stilts further up
an old man climbs the ladder with his lantern
its uncertain gleam can be descried
at a considerable distance
he himself in the loft
seems to be moving about among boxes
or shifting burdens of varying weights

X

All night along
the south face of the nearest moutnain
the glacier extends
its territorial interest

EMERGENT OCCASIONS

'A Little Journey to the Continent'

I *France*

Still there appeared to lurk some danger even in uncertainty.
Suddenly the broad sun rose over France.
I said, . . . look, the sun rises over France.
Our own perceptions are the world to us.
The ladies talked of dress and eating.
Many little villages ruined by the war
occupied the most romantic situations.
The postilion tells many lies.

II *Switzerland*

. . . a horrible spinet and a case of stuffed birds.
Before we sleep, however, we look out of window.
We consult on our situation.
The little Frenchman arrives with tubs and plums
and scissors and salt.
We stop at Loffenburgh and engage a boat for Mumpf;
the boat is small and frail, it requires much attention
to prevent an overset.

III *Germany*

In the morning, when we wake, we find we have been tied
all night to one island in the Rhine;
the wind changed against us immediately
on our departure the night before.

IV *Holland*

The country is flat but the hedges are pretty.

V *Italy*

Go to the Opera in the evening; we do not know
the name of it and cannot make out the story.
The singers are very good.

Go to the Opera in the evening;
the opera
we cannot hear, but the ballet
is very beautiful.

We see an excellent house, but out of repair,
with an excellent garden, but full of serpents.

A sirocco, but a pleasant evening.

A beautiful day, but not hot.
A cloudy day but a fine sunset.
A fine day,
though changeful as to clouds and wind.
A bad day, but a good sunset,
with a slight maestrale. In the evening
a heavy thunderstorm passed over.

—the most contemptible of lives,
is where you live in the world
and none of your passions or affections
are called into action.

. . . my boat of reeds.

And the evening *tutto sotto sopra*.

ORNITHOLOGICAL

In autumn the frill of the Great Crested Glebe is lost.

The nest of the Dabchick is a floating tangle
in a mere or similar haunt.

The Petrel lays one egg, white, faintly speckled
with rufous at the larger end.

At night the Manx Shearwater comes to land
at the breeding places with weird cooing cries and wails,
and shuffles to tunnels from which sepulchral, husky voices
coo 'kuk-kuk-hoo-coo.'

The food of the Fulmar is oily offal and refuse
fish and cuttles. It is a silent bird
except at the colonies, where a low cackling is heard
as the birds gape at one another with strange gestures.

In spring there is a white patch on the Cormorant's
thigh.

The Shag feeds on fish,
which it catches by diving
and swimming under water with great speed and with agile
twists and turns.

The Shelduck nests in a rabbit's burrow.

The Bittern's most outstanding note is a deep boom
which carries over a mile. This is uttered
with the bird's bill pointed
upward.

Like other drakes, the male Wigeon
has an 'eclipse' period in summer.

A silent bird, the Spoonbill very rarely
utters a low grunt.

. . . a pleasing whistle . . . a purring growl . . .
'honk' or 'agh' . . . 'Calloo' . . . 'pink-a-pink-a-pink'
. . . 'gobak, gobak'

Pale individuals appear among Buzzards.

The Brent Goose makes its nest
of a flat moss of vegetation and bits of bark or twig
and a smother of down; on the ground by water.

Even those of us who have not seen
the living bird are familiar with the sight
of Pheasants in poulterer's shops.

The toes of the Coot are lobed with webbing.

The Spotted Crake is very secretive and difficult to see.
The Water Rail is a very secretive bird and most difficult
to see. The corncrake is seldom seen, being in habit
very secretive.

The Dotterel is pathetically tame and unsuspecting.

Of the nuptial display of the Capercaillie,
various observers have heard notes which remind them
of the squalls of fighting cats,
of the drawing of corks,
and the sound of grinding knives.
The hens gather to listen to the song,
answering in excited
monosyllabic croaks.

Sometimes the nest of the Moorhen, of rushes and reeds,
lined with grass, is in a bush overhanging the water,
sometimes in the ground concealed in vegetation,
or in a tree.

The Mute Swan has barking notes and hisses when angry.

The song of the Skylark is too well known
to merit further description.

The song of the Stonechat resembles the click of pebbles.

On a still night the Turnstone's piping
rises as the tide disturbs the waders, and dies away
in the mystery of the dark ocean coastline.

DREAM CITIES

I City of Stone

Slabs
closed stone windows
staircases cut in
stone laterals
stone roofs with no need
of stones
echoes of stone on stone
stone shoes
the business of stone
moss on stone turning to

the stone woman through portals
gives birth to stone
Buddha eyelids

through stone lips
the oracle of stone
ejects to the pilgrim
the stone wafer

under stone trees in the Square
oblongs on squares at stone tables
each stone a solitude
(periodically
on the plain of stones
outside the city
squadrons of stones rise and fall)
each day a great wind comes
to polish each solitude

the yellow stone dish of the sun
the white stone cup of the moon

stone light is absence

beyond the plain of stones
the desert imagines glass

II City of Water

How the fountains celebrate the rain!
Inexhaustible indefatigable chalices caryatids of water
supporting downpouring flooding from cloud cisterns rivers
rush upward also through trees in the gulf of the city's
morning fog smokes from factory chimneys incense rises mist
in the sunken cathedral walls glisten damp with perpetual
prayers for the drowned along the rialto gondola smiles
business acquaintances plying on shores of back canals
washwomen bend over steaming basins wring their catch into
wharfside baskets hand it out in the rain-slick hands
of flowerwomen offer narcissi from other mirrors (lovers
with grotto eyes) a dowser ecstatic on every corner mermen
hawk pearls to tourists rumor: a caravan of whales
spouting approaches the city outside the city suburban oozy
dogs bark waterily in dripping gardens outdoors or indoors
cats continually shake their paws if a moon shone at night
a yellow waterlily attached to a rippling sky a new sun
rim of a shell aurora the harbor rocking so gently murmurs
rumors of peasants wading cityward hoisting above the waves
their one window of water in winter here rain falls six-sided
in spring trees sprout glass-green droplets when people weep
here they weep grains of sand fountains celebrate the rain

III City of Glass

Glint daz glit afar pierce need domes
towrs the traveller's eye goal chalce thyst
false dime paque spark clear struck
ester sili lime actual mark awns spun
wares heap ice rosy rads let cabbages ruta
merle transpar window finned scales early
breakrs play salt live shine jasp pearl
filtered false obelisk emirold Pliny mosques

Allah of stone into light-clash leioscopes d
from gleed child games pucks quirks cups
skirts no curtains chatter polde-do musick
clatter! sola railings stick walk messages
braille barometer envelopes brittleness of
translation painting on necessary reversal mirror
traffic almanac patience of flowers fountains
molten blown or rain yellow nugget white
lozenge night clustrs conversazioni transport
fusion fuschia in Squares glass birds sing glass songs
jet splinters sound saints fusion hexag
echoes of phalanx phials quoise cast anneal
mangan the millwheel to turn pulver slag sift
splinters sound sand

AMERICAN NOTES

I *California*

The old "forty-niners" passed through this sterile country
during the gold excitement.
The fact of the similarity of
the valleys led many astray, and they perished
from thirst. At the Pahrump Springs, a hardy
pioneer has settled in a lovely oasis and reared
a family. Those who have visited
say that away off there,
imprisoned by canyon walls and sandy deserts,
lives the most beautiful woman in the West.
Her fame for comeliness has spread rapidly since
civilization placed its foot in the Pahrump Valley,
which, by the way, has not made much progress.

II *North Dakota*

Over 210,000 tons of buffalo bones,
representing 7,800,000 animals,
have been exported from that state.

III *Virginia*

Mrs. Bouldin, who is engaged
in one of the Departments of Washington,
has sold for $500 the mahogany dining-table
formerly used by John Randolph, of Roanoke.

IV *Illinois*

Automatic nickel-in-the-slot
telephones have been introduced
experimentally in Chicago.

Designed to head off the "deadheads,"
the machines are provided with coin slots
for city, suburban, or long distance service.
Each coin rings a different bell
at the main office, and special operators
are employed to attend the machines.

V *California*

prospers apace. She ranks first among the States
in the production of grapes, almonds, walnuts,
oranges,honey, wine, and gold. She has paid out in bounties
$187,000 for the scalps of coyotes.

VI *New York*

H.M. Stanley has written to Major Pond, the well-known
concert agent, to say that he intends
visiting
the United States in the autumn,
and that he will have much
that is new to talk about.

VII *District of Columbia*

General Francis E. Spinner, pioneer advocate of women's
fitness for business employment at Washington,
where he was exceedingly popular, is to have
a statue.

IX *Rhode Island*

A bright summer is looked forward to at Newport,
where most of the cottages have been rented.
A number of permanent residents are making
extensive repairs to their property.
The thaw, when the Chateau-Sur-Mer lay empty,

caused hair-line cracks in the system to widen and burst,
and water poured down the marble lips of the staircase.
The chandelier sank from the painted ceiling,
the plinths of the hall pillars stood awash like piers.
A native observer, cupping his vision,
reported a small flounder swimming the travertine floors.
Then the caretaker, briefly absent, returned,
and ice entered in to the heart of the house,
began without haste to descend the stair.
At the approach of the glittering breath,
the arctic regard, the glacial fingers,
the chandelier's rigging thickened its crystal,
the flounder struggled and froze in an island sea,
scales, flesh, bony armature,
the tiny, cold moon of his eye,
the platinum ring in his throat.
Estimates of the cost of restoration
were predictably astronomical,
but now it appears that the alterations
will succeed in enhancing the total effect.

X *New Jersey*

Coaching excursions
will be established soon by a syndicate made up of
millionaire "whips." The route, 100 miles in length,
will go through Trenton, Princeton, New Brunswick,
and Newark. There will be seventeen relays on every trip,
each coach using seventy horses. The object is
the development of coaching, and the projectors
do not anticipate any profit
from the venture.

XI *New York*

Mr. Edward Parker Deacon is at present a prominent
figure in New York society.
His shooting episode at Nice is now
only referred to in whispers. His wife,
who was the cause of the disaster,
resides in London.

XII *Massachusetts*

Business men give it as their opinion
that Boston has suffered
less from the late "hard times" than any other
Eastern city. It is quite flourishing and brisk,
whereas Philadelphia, and Chicago,
were loud in their complaints.
Matters are mending everywhere.

XIII *California*

Mr. Slevin, LL.D., in a lecture on the origin
of the name California, explained
that it was first used in a work on Spanish chivalry,
published in 1510. This work,
an alleged history of the adventures of
Amadis of Gaul and his son Esplandian, was of great length,
and divided into a large number of short stories,
one of which was the manner in which "Califla,
the Queen of the island of California,
a country inhabited only by women, who lived as Amazons
and had gold without end," saved Constantinople
from an attack by the Persians.
This story was widely read by the people of Spain,
and by many regarded as fact. Among the believers
were members of Cortez' expedition, who, upon landing
upon the peninsula of
Lower California, imagined
they were on an island, which, owing to its apparent
riches, they named
after the fabled isle, and Cortez himself
called the new country
"California."

NOTES FROM THE VOYAGE

i

In the tall building nubilous windowed echoing
vox humana lapped trilateral footing heaped pavilions
auricles in the mass exchanged towards chance
identities stamped immigration outward bound
we pass the barrier and the line moves up
hundreds have signed on parting with thousands
lured by advertisements the gloss "for once"
nobody mentions icebergs nobody mentions drowning
under the canopy flashes of blue ice
record our crossing this May afternoon
the little bridge that separates who must remain
from those who enter the Leviathan.

ii

Sleek in her hugeness trailing empressive plumes
offal and oily refuse at her rim
baskets of roses in her vestibule
six hour turnaround Moscow wedding palace
only the tremor in her depths betrays
modification of the imperturbable
horizon we stroll on deck and sip champagne
and comment on the streamers and the band
at the port rail a siren all in white
hat veil dress stockings shoes of purest white
leans out exalted laughing rather tight
and scatters white-gloved kisses to the multitude.

iii

The blast explodes the wheel of harbor gulls
sets the whole city back
towers blocks spires
reel in the gape of azure violence
what is the matter oh what is the matter
the fissure folded in the missed pulse found
the sky resumes itself assimilates
apprehension bandaged by smiles

pale discs of littoral faces on the dock
begin their slow inevitable slide
past farewells nudged by bridesmaids urged
by bells the great anachronism sails.

iv

At eight o'clock we give up liberty
glide under that narrow verifiable span
when we come to it city and islands
sunk with their lights behind us oceanwards
remnants at dusk of a substantial realm
scarcely a trace of it in the deepening blue
("It's you," "No, it's you")
the evening the evening out we are chained to
each other by innumerable hours to be spent
in bars pools casinos miniature golf
religious services anything to distract
from the engulfing fiction of the initial act.

v

Nobody anybody goes to boat drill.

vi

Informal sitting lady from Buffalo in vermeil
silent spouse the siren with a Stetsoned male
in her eyes echoes of cocaine that radiance
a German expert in cement
firm in Florida reverts to Prussian when the waiter
mistakes his order of tomato soup for juice
of lamb for ham raps out questions: "Oh, I am
supposed to apologize? I was in the wrong?"
Buffalo croon, "It was only natural . . ."
the wife sealed in gray waiter considers
jumping overboard our fragile raft trembles
under star-seeded skies in the red saloon.

vii

The first night of course we don't dress
go down in the elevator thirteen stories to levitate
in the privacy of our cabin we hardly know
the difference between land and sea

dither in yaw and spin the hiss and roil
of the real Atlantic getting under weigh
outside the open porthole no more to us
than singing telephone wires back in Kansas
reach out and touch ("Oh, to whom?")
eyeless creatures in the depths coiling
boneless limbs caught in the toil of the salt-
seeded sea brought up plosive alive.

viii

Nothing we declare nothing
never has there been anything
like it under the sun the morning sea unfurling
proud arched as the necks of horses plunging
rearing tumultuous tumbling
mere limitless motion manes flying
lunging playful expansive as whales curving
cursive apostrophic leaping re-entering
tumid contiguous wet umbrageous glittering
energy bruising unfailing stinging unyielding
caving hurled like chariots over the unbesmirched
fair far surface under the speeding sky.

ix

Velleities. Oddities. Quiddities. These
cockleshell quadragenarians pocketbook-carrying
husbands followed at prescribed
intervals oleaginous physiognomies wives
"I did get it in the end but it wasn't
simple" billows like mohair scarves from orange-brown
worked skins hennaed bereted attenuated
"Scatter my ashes, strew them on the air"
a festival of life and on the foredeck signs
of heavy weather we have heard of on the wireless.

x

Awaking to grisaille
a waste of waters wavering with change
few passengers to lunch fewer to dinner
the furniture constrained like animals
Iocusque goes under Icarus in seasmoke

peaks troughs ruck rubble ruin and again
ruin spate snags hollows no rote here
winding sheet after sheet of wind brute wallowing
streaming with foam tatters each Niagara
shuddering first class drenched in cologne
in the hold two coffins shift in the swell
subside for better or worse once and for all.

xi

Tucked up in chairs in blankets
we convalesce accept
ministrations cups of strengthening
oolong we do
not look at each other but at our wake
drowse gazing at the watersilk
cloak spread for our queening
weakly imagine dolphins kindly creatures bearing
the tender spirits of the dead to Blessed Isles
two thousand miles from land our behemoth
browses her meadow as if she did not know
the pale enormous distance still to go.

xii

Tristesse, tristesse! And so to break
the monotony we have
the Daily Raffle Turkish and Sauna Baths
Boaters and Feathers prior to the Show
Capo di Monte Lynda Gloria Tyme for Men
a reward offered for the return
of a small blue purse to Mrs. Foshee
(Cabin 4116) Pet Competition Hobby Arts
Gentlemen's Table Tennis Tournament
Tote on the Ship's Run Duty Free
Children's Fancy Dress Parade and Captain Dick
Diver's Next-to-Last Night Masquerade.

xiii

Rouge ruffles Patagonian decor
papier-mâché glyptodonts rocks thoroacuses
guanacoes manadoroes Sultans mandarins
Mrs Foshee traces of weeping mascara

mermaid siren in green scales twists
with male orca coruscating fin dorsal
beneath incongrous chandeliers in the Grand Concourse
the band pumps pumps pumps
under the din for your leisure and pleasure
fin de siècle finesse of the body
corporeal cells ages raging to dance
disguised degaussed de gustibus dance!

xiv

"Is it you?" "Is it you?"

xv

Consider the delicate fabrications of our bodies
subtle articulations intricate canals
contractile membranes nervous ganglia
intimate aspirations in the lungs' rosy chambers
consider the heart's clenched fist
how on every voyage there is one sensing
the iceberg's breath at the salt-glazed window
who jettisons apparatus launches himself
into the roaring of unstanched waterfalls
underwater rambling with piscine irides
bones hulls rials brachia woven with bright weeds.

xvi

A body moving through the dark
the lifelong marriage of the light and dark
the long divorce of dark from light
divergence of the light from dark to darkened light
justification of the lines
of demarcation towards dawn the slippage
like the ring on a finger of land towards sea
the sight of tall houses washed with the color of
flesh at sunrise coming towards us easing in
to the harbor to disembark finally with our impedimenta
and walk separately in double file
through gates of custom to the old new world.

INDEX OF TITLES

INDEX OF FIRST LINES